Kings of t

Michael Clower is the author of three bestselling racing books: *Mick Kinane – Big Race King*, which was *Sporting Life*'s racing book of the year, *Champion Charlie* and *The Legend of Istabraq*. Born in Sussex and educated at Shrewsbury, he went to Kenya to begin his journalistic career with the *East African Standard* and rode as an amateur against the professionals on the Flat before moving to Ireland. For more than 25 years he was one of the country's leading racing journalists. He was the Irish correspondent of the *Sporting Life* and wrote for the *Racing Post*. He was also Irish racing correspondent for both the *Sunday Times* and the *Sunday Mirror*. He and his wife Tessa now live near Cape Town where he is the South African correspondent of *The Irish Field*.

ALSO BY MICHAEL CLOWER

Mick Kinane – Big Race King
Champion Charlie
The Legend of Istabraq
Kenya Turf Guide

Kings of the Turf

Ireland's Top Racehorse Trainers

Michael Clower

First published 2007 by Aurum Press Limited
7 Greenland Street
London NW1 0ND
www.aurumpress.co.uk

This paperback edition was first published in 2008 by Aurum Press.

A catalogue record for this book is available from the British Library.

ISBN 978 1 84513 364 1

10 9 8 7 6 5 4 3 2 1
2012 2011 2010 2009 2008

Typeset in Minion by SX Composing DTP, Rayleigh, Essex
Printed and bound in Great Britain by
Creative Print and Design, Blaina, Wales

CONTENTS

ACKNOWLEDGEMENTS

The lists of biggest races won comprise primarily Group One races on the Flat and races at the Cheltenham Festival. The Grand National, Irish National, Galway Plate and Galway Hurdle are also automatic inclusions; others have been added as considered appropriate.

My thanks are due to Claire Barry, Peadar Flanagan, Ryan McElligott, Martin Murphy, Bryan Pugh and John Randall for assistance in helping to check various facts. I am also indebted to Peter Mooney who supplied the photographs.

PREFACE TO THE PAPERBACK EDITION

A lot happens in racing in twelve months and the event that made the most headlines was the collapse of the case against Kieren Fallon at the Old Bailey in December 2007. Fallon, along with others, was charged with conspiracy to defraud and the trial began on the day after he put up an inspired performance on Dylan Thomas in the Prix de l'Arc de Triomphe. However, the evidence against him looked increasingly weak and inadequate. All the accused were acquitted by the jury on the direction of the judge who said that there was no case to answer.

The cost to Fallon, both financially and emotionally, was enormous – but there was more to come. Less than 24 hours after the verdict, news broke that he had tested positive (for a substance reported to be cocaine) after winning a big race in France the previous August. In January 2008 the French racing authorities banned him from riding anywhere in the world for 18 months, and Johnny Murtagh was promptly appointed his successor at Ballydoyle.

Aidan O'Brien and his new jockey set about taking racing by storm and by the end of Royal Ascot in June the stable had chalked up an incredible 11 Group One winners. They were not the only ones to reach new heights. Jim Bolger, pinning his faith on Galileo as a stallion, has been rewarded with some outstanding successes, notably with New Approach.

New Approach (Kevin Manning) comes from a long way back to win the 2008
Derby for Jim Bolger (Getty Images)

This colt, unbeaten as a two-year-old, may have been unable to
match O'Brien's Henrythenavigator in both the English and Irish
2,000 Guineas, but he put up an extraordinary performance when
winning the Derby. For much of the race he fought for his head and
he turned for home almost impossibly far back. Either would be the
kiss of death for any normal horse but this one was still full of
running. He then found his path blocked by a wall of horses, but rider
Kevin Manning spotted an opening on the inner and his mount
powered through it.

Unfortunately, Bolger's late decision to go for the turf's Blue
Riband upset both the ante-post market and a number of the British
press, and the resulting controversy rather overshadowed New
Approach's amazing victory.

An update to the lists of each the trainer's biggest wins can be found
in an appendix at the end of this book (page 208).

Michael Clower
June 2008

INTRODUCTION

The first few years of the twenty-first century have turned into a golden era for Irish racing. The quality of the country's racehorses is so high that record numbers of winners have been notched up at the Cheltenham Festival, while victory in the major European Flat races has become an accepted part of racing life.

Ireland's trainers have been able to attract wealthy patrons and many of the best bred horses in the world, preparing them for victory at the highest level across Europe and beyond. They have become one of the most successful elements of the transformation of the Irish economy known as the Celtic Tiger. But their achievement, almost alone among a sea of entrepreneurs, is only marginally due to the huge amounts of money that the European Union has poured into Ireland.

The upsurge in trainers' fortunes, particularly those training horses for racing over jumps, is a direct result of the Irish government's decision to inject the entire income from taxation of off-course betting into the racing and greyhound industries. Prize money has spiralled in consequence, making the ordinary Irish race worth more than its British counterpart and providing the owners of the best jumpers with such handsome rewards that they no longer have to sell their animals to make ends meet. Not only are the best Irish jump horses now kept in Ireland, but trainers across the water, cut off from their previous steady stream of potential stars, find themselves going into battle with what is effectively a second eleven. Furthermore, they are up against teams that are world class.

It's much the same story in Flat racing, although for different reasons. True, the big prize money increase has been important, but not so important as John Magnier's decision to run the Ballydoyle racing operation at more than twice the scale it was in Vincent O'Brien's heyday. Furthermore, the Aga Khan, who used to have horses in Britain but not in Ireland, now puts a substantial proportion of his superbly bred racehorses into training on The Curragh.

Success in racing tends to go in cycles. For a time, France, with its Tote monopoly providing high levels of prize money, had the best Flat horses. Britain, whose racing operation is far bigger than that in Ireland, has otherwise tended to be the principal European superpower, whereas the Emerald Isle has experienced only brief periods at the top of the table. For instance, more than fifty years went by between the first Derby winner trained in Ireland (Orby in 1906) and the second. There were five Irish-trained Derby winners between 1962 and 1972, but a sixteen-year gap between Secreto's triumph in 1984 and Sinndar's millennium victory.

The infrequent highs, and lengthy lows, are even more clearly exemplified by the Grand National. Just under a century ago the world's greatest steeplechase was won three years on the trot by Irish-trained horses, but this proved to be a brief purple patch not matched until Vincent O'Brien won with Early Mist, Royal Tan and Quare Times in the 1950s. L'Escargot in 1975 was the first Irish-trained winner for seventeen years, and there was not another until Bobbyjo twenty-four years later. However, in the last decade the picture has changed completely with Bobbyjo paving the way for Papillon, Monty's Pass, Hedgehunter, Numbersixvalverde and Silver Birch.

Winning outside Ireland has long been the key indicator. Victories at home are important, but success in the prestige overseas races tends to be valued more highly. Such has been the achievement of Irish trainers in recent years that some modern racegoers, and pundits too, seem to think that never before have home-trained horses won such a large proportion of the big British races. They were not around in 1958 when the three days of the Cheltenham Festival witnessed eight Irish winners, a record that stood for almost half a century. In 1977 there were seven, almost as big a cause for celebration as the double figure score of 2006, taking into account the much smaller number of races at the meeting.

Royal Ascot has also seen some huge Irish hauls, with seven winners in both 1975 and 1977. Vincent O'Brien was responsible for nearly two-thirds of these successes, but he was not the only thorn in the British side. In the 1960s Paddy Prendergast's sorties across the water were so many and so fruitful that he ended up champion trainer in Britain three years running. Just to rub salt into the wound, O'Brien took the title the following season.

But one thing that sets the present golden spell apart from its predecessors is that the big race victories are spread among a much larger number of trainers. Tom Dreaper towered over his rivals in the glory days of Arkle and Flyingbolt, and after O'Brien had elected to concentrate on the Flat, whereas today there are more than a dozen stables housing Cheltenham winners. Racing on the Flat, particularly at the top level, is concentrated among fewer trainers but still more than was the case thirty or forty years ago. And with good reason.

Racing in Ireland is now a much bigger industry. The number of horses in training has more than doubled, and there has been a fifty per cent increase in the number of races. Training racehorses has become far more profitable and, as a result, appeals as an occupation to a significantly greater number of people.

This book is devoted to a dozen trainers at the top of their profession today. The majority of the twelve picked themselves by virtue of their outstanding success. Choosing the remainder from the many obvious candidates has been problematical and has resulted in the omission of several deserving cases. The author is well aware that his selection may not meet with universal agreement, but the purpose of the book is to get behind the outward persona of each trainer and find out what has moulded their characters, as well as what makes them tick – and makes them more successful than the vast majority of their rivals.

I

AIDAN O'BRIEN

October 1994. Vincent O'Brien retires after more than half a century of turning out big race winners, having built a reputation as perhaps the greatest racehorse trainer there has ever been. The tributes, on television and in the newspapers, are lavish. Two of the most widely used words are *legendary* and *incomparable*.

No one expected that O'Brien would soon have to make do with legendary, let alone see his achievements facing an almost unstoppable challenge from the shy, pale-faced bespectacled young man who succeeded him at Ballydoyle. Yet Aidan O'Brien (no relation to his predecessor) promptly set about rolling back most of the established boundaries of training achievement, and he has rewritten the record books in the process. He may be a quiet and reserved character, but there is a steely determination to succeed cloaked beneath that unassuming manner. He also has an uncanny knack of being able to understand horses like few others before him, and of moulding their minds. This, coupled with his extraordinary dedication, has enabled him to build up a big race record that threatens to engulf those of the outstanding trainers of previous centuries, not just in Europe but around the globe.

Born on 16 October 1969, Aidan was brought up on a farm near Clonroche in County Wexford, the third of six children of Denis and Stella O'Brien. The farm has been in the family for generations and his mother also came from farming stock. His paternal grandfather kept half-bred horses, but Denis switched to thoroughbreds, riding and training his own horses in point-to-points. Denis calculates that he won 140 races, 'although it wasn't as hard to win in those days and the breeding wasn't as hot either'. He also rode a few winners on the racecourse in bumpers (amateur flat races) and over hurdles, but was too heavy to make further progress.

As a teenager Aidan had ambitions to become a trainer, and when he left school he took over the six point-to-pointers on the farm. However, he did not exactly meet with instant success and in his initial season he failed to get a single one of them to the racecourse. His father was not surprised: 'Everything went wrong, but that's usually what happens. Training is a tough game.'

Denis O'Brien found his son a job picking strawberries and, when the fruit season was over, another in the mill in Clonroche working for the Co-op. He started at the bottom, sweeping the floor, and had been promoted to driving a fork-lift truck by the time he decided to try racing again and had joined the stables of P.J. Finn on The Curragh in County Kildare.

However, Finn, son of the legendary Tipperary hurling captain Jimmy Finn, was on the move and he closed down his Curragh operation only two months after O'Brien joined him. Next stop was Coolcullen, high in the County Carlow hills, where Jim Bolger has a highly successful Flat-racing stable. The hard-working Bolger runs a tight ship and has a reputation for expecting plenty from his staff, but the seventeen-year-old O'Brien relished the life. His father sometimes worried about the hours his son put in, particularly since he had a long drive to and from work each day, but this was a solid grounding for what was to become O'Brien's chosen way of life:

I started work in the dark and I finished in the dark. I went there as a stable lad and I thought I could learn a lot from Jim. For the first three weeks I was not even allowed to ride out, but by the time I left three and a half years later, I had progressed to such an extent that I did not have any stable yard duties. I did just about everything there. Jim expects the best from you all the time, but if you give it to him, he is good to you.

Bolger, with whom champion jump jockey Tony McCoy started his race-riding career, was impressed with the young O'Brien's willingness to work and learn. He gave him opportunities on the racecourse and O'Brien soon became a particularly competent amateur jockey.

O'Brien was nineteen when he rode in a bumper at the 1989 Galway Festival for Bolger on a horse called Midsummer Fun. Down at the start, his attention was caught by a dark-haired girl who was also riding in the race. O'Brien duly won, and Anne Marie Crowley, a part-time model and the eldest of Joe Crowley's six daughters, finished fifth on a horse trained by her father. Not long afterwards, O'Brien asked her out. At the beginning of 1991 Crowley handed over his training permit to Anne Marie, who traded it in for a full licence, and in August that year O'Brien left Bolger to help his future wife at their yard at Piltown, County Kilkenny. His former employer was sad to part with such a good worker, who was by this stage one of his assistants. He famously remarked, 'I would have done anything to keep Aidan, bar marry him!'

O'Brien and Anne Marie became a wonderfully successful partnership and in the 1992/93 season she was Ireland's first woman champion jumps trainer. She also became a mother for the first time and her husband took over the licence. He worked even harder than he had done at Bolger's. He was up at 6.30 a.m., feeding every horse in the yard, and did the lunchtime and evening feeds as well whenever he was not away racing. He seldom finished his rounds of the horses before ten at night and often it was nearer midnight.

He and his wife built a new stable block which incorporated the house where they lived. They also built the stiffest gallop in the country. The soon-to-be-famous Piltown hill is a one-mile shavings all-weather gallop, which is on the collar the whole way. Curving to the right all the time, it stretches up the side of the hill, rising 300 feet over the first seven furlongs with an even steeper climb for the final furlong. O'Brien got the idea from Bolger, but the gallop at Coolcullen rises by only half as much. Such gallops make a lot of sense for National Hunt horses, whose legs and tendons are often suspect. It takes less work to get them fit and they do not have to gallop as fast.

O'Brien's results were incredible. He was champion jumps trainer in his first season, 1993/94, setting a new prize money record, and became the only Irish trainer ever to send out 100 winners in his first year. For good measure, he was also champion amateur rider.

His father-in-law looked on, bemused and occasionally annoyed. 'I could tell he was going to be good from the first time he came here,' Joe Crowley recalls. 'Being an old fellow, I didn't agree with everything he did and we clashed a few times. But, generally speaking, I tried to keep my mouth shut and let him do it his way. A lot of the things he did were proved right over time.'

One of these was O'Brien's practice of running horses far more often than other trainers. The fact that his horses were supremely fit played its part in enabling him to do this, but he was also a big believer in correcting the dehydration caused by racing with the use of electrolytes. They are salts given in the feed and they replace the body salts a horse loses in a race. They also contain vitamins C and E, as well as protein. O'Brien would closely monitor his horses' liquid intake:

I would know exactly how much each horse drank and how much it needed to put back after a hard piece of work. I would be told how much they had drunk after a race and, once they were home, I could measure how much they drank by the level of their water bowls. Once they put the liquid back, my view was why not run them again in a day or two? Often the race would have taken no more out of them than the hill would. Horses are happier kept on the go. If you took the weekend off, you might not feel like going back to work on Monday. You would be better to keep working! It's the same with horses.

Even at that early stage O'Brien was not short of ambition. In an interview with *The Sporting Life* he revealed that his aim was to win Group One races, 'including the Derby, and I also want to win the Cheltenham Gold Cup'.

But success came at a price. Longer-established trainers found it hard to become accustomed to someone who looked like a teenager sweeping the board and collecting huge prize money that should have been theirs. Irish racing has its fair share of gossips and rumour-mongers, many of them driven by jealousy, and stories that it was really Joe Crowley who was doing the training found receptive ears. Another story going the rounds was that O'Brien was so successful because he trained 300 horses. The knockers irritated O'Brien and amused Crowley, who never wanted more than a dozen horses all the time he held a permit.

One man who heard the rumours and immediately dismissed them was John Magnier. When Vincent O'Brien announced his retirement in 1994, his son-in-law wasted little time in inviting the new O'Brien to move his operation to Ballydoyle, the magnificent County Tipperary training establishment where Vincent trained most of his big race winners. 'Aidan O'Brien was the worst-kept secret in Ireland,' Magnier was fond of saying a few years later when O'Brien was winning all before him at the highest level.

Representatives of Magnier's Coolmore Stud operation said at the time that the intention was to turn Ballydoyle, and its magnificent gallops, into a training centre for various trainers, but O'Brien was the only one to receive an invitation to occupy the place. When the answer was yes, Magnier expected the man who was still a few days short of his twenty-fifth birthday to concentrate on the bluebloods at Ballydoyle. He was surprised to discover that Vincent's replacement intended simply to add these horses to the battalion at Piltown, and work an even longer day than before. Piltown to Ballydoyle was a fifty-mile round trip and he would make the journey every day, often twice.

> I was simply asked if I would be interested in leasing the stables and the gallops and, frankly, I felt it was an honour to be asked. I knew it would mean splitting the operation but I didn't regard that as any big deal. After all, my operation at Piltown was split between three yards with sixty horses in the main yard, twelve at Joe's place and another twelve or so in a converted barn not far from the gallops. Some people might have thought I was stretching myself a bit, although I certainly didn't look at it that way. Obviously the gallops were different from those at Piltown but you just adjust the horses' training schedules accordingly.

O'Brien soon became almost as effective a force on the Flat as he was over jumps and, as Ballydoyle took up more and more of his time, he and Anne Marie moved their rapidly expanding family to a bungalow previously occupied by Vincent's eldest daughter, Elizabeth McClory. It was not until 2004 that they took over their predecessor's house adjoining the main yard.

In 1995 O'Brien became the first trainer to send out the first three horses in the Galway Plate and, as if to demonstrate both the strength in depth of his two-year-olds and his ability with them, he made a huge assault on the valuable Tattersalls Breeders Stakes at The Curragh a month later. He was responsible for nine of the twenty-nine runners and four of the first five places, and took almost eighty per cent of the prize money. He also won three other races that day, to complete his first four-timer. O'Brien went on to become the first trainer in Ireland to send out 200 winners in a year.

But this was only the beginning. The following year he had his first Cheltenham success with Urubande and in 1997 his first Royal Ascot winner. That year, far more sensationally, he also won each of the first three Irish classics. Even Magnier was impressed. He has made himself one of the wealthiest men in Ireland by selecting high-class racehorses to make the grade as stallions and building up Coolmore into the world's pre-eminent stallion station. In Vincent O'Brien's heyday, it had been Magnier's practice to take a share in many of the horses, and Aidan O'Brien's phenomenal success rate persuaded him to multiply his investment several times over. Partnered by former bookmaker Michael Tabor, he began buying more and more of the best-bred yearlings at the world's top auction sales and putting them into training at Ballydoyle.

Magnier questioned the young maestro when O'Brien wanted to run two or three horses in the top races. Vincent O'Brien never did this because he took the view that only one of them could win and defeat would devalue the others. His successor reasoned that 'the more we run, the more chance we have of winning. Also it's good for horses to race. Horses that run consistently at the top level are the ones that make stallions, and I don't think it does any horse any harm to get beaten.' Like Joe Crowley before him, Magnier learnt to defer to the younger man's wishes and was rewarded with a string of champions who went on to earn him a fortune at stud.

Magnier has done well out of O'Brien. It was a tremendous leap of faith to invest so much money in one young man's ability, but almost every year the trainer has succeeded in turning superbly bred horses into racehorses of the highest class who become worth so much that the operation pays for itself several times over. Many of the horses Magnier put into training have been by Sadler's Wells, by far Coolmore's biggest earner and most successful stallion. O'Brien is impressed with the quality of the horse's progeny: 'They are all hardy, tough sorts and have a consistent level. A lot of horses are morning glories – they are good at home and they let you down when they go to the racecourse – but the offspring of Sadler's Wells are not.'

King Of Kings was by Sadler's Wells and he followed up a brilliant two-year-old career by giving O'Brien his first English classic success in the 2,000 Guineas in 1998. That year Istabraq won his first Champion Hurdle and O'Brien became champion National Hunt trainer for the fifth and final time. By August his sister-in-law, Frances Crowley, had taken over at Piltown and his own involvement with jumpers was restricted to Istabraq and a handful of others, all at Ballydoyle. But the trainer's dedication intensified. He had special closed-circuit television installed and from his home would watch Istabraq and the other top horses as they dozed in their stables.

In 1999 Aidan O'Brien became Ireland's champion Flat race trainer for the first time, and he has headed the prize money table in every subsequent season. The following year Istabraq won his third consecutive Champion Hurdle and Giant's Causeway won five Group One races. This extraordinary chestnut, with white socks on his nearside legs and a long white blaze extending to his left nostril, loved getting into a battle. Time and time again he would allow his principal opponent to draw alongside. You could see him then look across at the other horse and, as if saying 'This is as near as you are going to get, laddie,' he would dig that little bit deeper to go on and win his race. Little wonder that he became known as 'The Iron Horse'.

However, even the magnificent millennium season was put in the shade by the successes of 2001. That year O'Brien set a new world record of twenty-three Group One wins, including seven classic victories, notably the Derby with Galileo, while Johannesburg won all his seven starts, including the Breeders' Cup Juvenile in New York, to entitle him to be called the world's champion two-year-old. The colt's trainer became the first based overseas to win the Flat trainers' championship in Britain since his namesake twenty-four years earlier.

O'Brien repeated that feat the following year, even though his number of Group One victories was 'only' nineteen, but they did include high-profile wins with Rock Of Gibraltar, in the colours of Sir Alex Ferguson, and a second Derby with High Chaparral, who went on to win the Irish Derby and the Breeders' Cup Turf.

Vincent O'Brien won the Derby six times and so his successor still has some way to go, but he seems to be alive to the challenge posed by this formidable race which many still regard as the greatest prize racing has to offer: 'The Derby is a very difficult race to win and it's probably the ultimate test. Your horse has to have both speed and stamina, and he has to have great balance to be able to handle the terrain. At the same time it's important to look past the Derby.'

O'Brien is referring to all the rich prizes in the remainder of the season, but the esteem in which he holds the Derby is illustrated by his massive assault on the 2007 race. He ran eight horses – no trainer in the race's long history has ever run as many – although second-placed Eagle Mountain was the only Ballydoyle runner in the first four.

In 2003 O'Brien suffered the beginning of a downward spiral that was to have headline-making repercussions. The number of his Group One winners dropped to nine, even though he won six of the ten in Ireland, the St Leger with Brian Boru and another Breeders' Cup race with High Chaparral, when Mick Kinane rode one of the best races of his long career to dead-heat for the valuable prize.

Ironically, Kinane had just learnt that he was to lose his job as first jockey at Ballydoyle, though the news did not break until thirteen days later when it was revealed that Jamie Spencer would replace him the following season. Kinane had held the post, the best in racing, since the start of the 1999 season and had ridden many of the stable's big race winners outside Ireland in the previous two seasons. However, his relationship with O'Brien was entirely professional and O'Brien was never all that keen on him going to Ballydoyle to ride work. As a result, Kinane sometimes found himself picking the wrong one when the stable ran more than one horse in big races.

Magnier and Tabor, a particular fan of Kinane's riding, would have been happy to continue with him, and significantly it was Kinane the stable turned to once more when Kieren Fallon was barred from riding in Britain part-way through the 2006 season. But at the end of 2003 O'Brien wanted Spencer, who had ridden Brian Boru to victory in the St Leger.

The switch proved to be a disaster. Spencer is a naturally talented rider with a flair for taking risks, and he often brings off improbable victories as a result. He has a fondness for dropping horses right out and then delivering them with a decisive late run. But his early days as stable jockey at Ballydoyle were marred by a series of suspensions, usually as a result of failing to keep his mounts straight in the closing stages of a race. There were also problems with the horses. The general level was not as good as in previous seasons and one of the best of them, Yeats, who was ante-post favourite for the 2004 Derby, had to be withdrawn a few days before the race with muscle problems.

The Spencer era reached a controversial low point in Chicago in August 2004 when Powerscourt finished first in the Arlington Million, only to be disqualified for swerving violently across the other runners when he hit the front. Spencer, who had his whip in his wrong hand and made no attempt to switch it, admitted his mistake but the damage had been done. From that point on, many racing journalists, particularly those based in Britain, were critical of Spencer's riding. When he was beaten on all his Breeders' Cup mounts, he was vilified. The stable finished the year with just three Group One successes, its lowest haul since Magnier began to increase his investment.

To his credit, O'Brien remained loyal (the cynics said he had no choice – he could hardly sack two jockeys in little more than twelve months) and instead tried to correct some of Spencer's faults. Early the following season, he made it clear to his jockey that he wanted him more and more at Ballydoyle in order to put in as much time as possible with the horses. For Spencer, the steadily mounting pressure from his boss, on top of all that press criticism, was too great a cross to bear. Words were spoken, he walked out and refused to go back. In some ways it was the making of Spencer. He picked himself up and, to widespread amazement, set about riding as many winners as he could, and for as many different trainers as possible, with the avowed intention of becoming champion jockey in Britain. It says much for

Jamie Spencer's character, as well as for his talent, that he succeeded at the first attempt.

The walk-out was intensely embarrassing for O'Brien, not least because racing's rumour mill suggested that the split was due as much to the flaws in his own make-up as to those in Spencer's. Magnier and Tabor turned to Kieren Fallon, an outstanding rider but a man more of Kinane's vintage than Spencer's, and a jockey whose brilliance on horses was to a considerable extent negated by the well-publicised problems he ran into once he got off them. Significantly, Magnier made the appointment himself and O'Brien was brought into the discussions by phone, at Fallon's request, only once the basic terms had been agreed.

However, O'Brien quickly came to appreciate his new jockey. Fallon wanted to put in every spare moment getting to know the horses at Ballydoyle, and he had valuable insights to offer on the sort of races they could win. The new partnership got off to a dream start when they won both Newmarket Guineas races with Footstepsinthesand and Virginia Waters. After six more Group One victories, Ballydoyle won both the St Leger and the Irish Champion Stakes on a memorable day in September. O'Brien finished the season once more as champion trainer in both Ireland and Britain.

There has been some surprise that O'Brien has not set up on his own, rather than remain as a private trainer to Magnier and his business partners. Ballydoyle gives him the considerable advantage of being able to train the best horses in the world with the aid of some of the best facilities, but the drawback is that he is not his own boss. His reputation is now so huge – and it stretches right round the racing globe – that he could attract the highest level of patronage, plus million-pound horses, if he decided to set up his own training establishment. He would have the means to buy his own place too because he has earned a considerable amount of money from his percentage of the prize money he has won. True, he has not had to worry about attracting owners or managing the stable's finances – a dual burden for most trainers – but his success rate would look after the former and any competent accountant could ensure that the bills were paid.

The pressure of working for men with high standards, accustomed to achieving results, would also be less if O'Brien was the man in overall control, but for the moment he seems to prefer a situation where he can concentrate on what he does best: getting the utmost out of his horses. He also has his own way of coping with pressures and setbacks:

> There are times when I feel anxious but we all [at Ballydoyle] do our best. In a race it's the jockey's responsibility to get it right but I know that sometimes things are going to go wrong. When things go bad, I find it easier to sleep. I simply look forward to the next day and I then try to make that day last as long as I can.

On the racecourse O'Brien is quiet and unassuming. He normally reveals his true feelings only in the winner's enclosure, when he will speak about his horses with passion and intensity. At other times he is guarded about what he says, as if he fears that his words will be taken down and used against him in the following day's papers. He is also surprisingly reticent about outlining plans for his horses. Occasionally he lets slip that this is because of the letters he has received from irate punters who have backed his horses ante-post in races he said they would go for, only to see their cash go down the drain when he changed his mind.

This reluctance to commit himself is regarded as a weakness by those of his rivals who have no such compunction, while others point to his apparent dread of putting his head above the parapet when controversy arises. When the row blew up between Magnier and Sir Alex Ferguson over the ownership of Rock Of Gibraltar, for example, O'Brien's silence was deafening.

One of the rare occasions on which O'Brien did speak out came after George Washington won the 2006 Queen Elizabeth II Stakes, and Frankie Dettori complained to the stewards that his mount had been carried wide by Seamus Heffernan on the Ballydoyle-trained Ivan Denisovich. The Ascot stewards gave Heffernan a fourteen-day suspension for improper riding, although this was reduced on appeal to six days for careless riding.

'I tried to talk to Frankie after the race, but all he was interested in was shouting and hurling abuse at me,' said O'Brien. 'When everything goes right, Frankie is great but on Saturday, when things didn't work out for him, he had to blame someone. That someone was Seamus. Frankie threw the toys out of the pram like a spoilt child.'

O'Brien speaks so quietly that it can often be hard to hear what he is saying, particularly in packed winner's enclosures, and it's the same on the phone. This all adds to the impression of his being a meek and mild man. But it can be a false impression. Journalists he considers to have overstepped the mark have discovered this to their cost, as have some of his staff. 'Sometimes he can get rattled,' says Charlie Swan, who rode for him over jumps. 'If somebody takes a horse up the gallop too fast, for instance, he will really give it to them.'

Swan has given a lot of thought to why O'Brien is so successful and he believes he has found the answer:

Horses enjoy life in his care and he spends an awful lot of time with them. He has so many horses, it surprises me that he can recognise each one, but he does, and it's far more than simply recognising them. He has an intimate knowledge of every single one of them, and he is able to understand their individual characteristics. It's this understanding of horses, coupled with his total dedication, that makes him such a brilliant trainer.

Joe Crowley takes a similar view:

He has something different from other trainers, rather like a top footballer or hurler has that something different, plus the fact that if somebody else had the ability to do what Aidan does, they might go drinking or something else. Aidan has the dedication to go with his ability. He also knows how his horses' minds work, and how to mould their minds in the way that he wants.

O'Brien does not drink, not even a celebratory glass of champagne. Unlike other trainers, he does not have to spend time entertaining owners and recruiting new ones. He can spend every hour he is not away racing with his horses, and he does just that. Rarely does he take a day off, let alone a holiday.

Few trainers, other than those whose operations are so small that they do most of the work themselves, spend so much time in their yards. In the process O'Brien learns about each horse's individual likes and dislikes, and what to do about them. This is not to say that other trainers would benefit by doing the same, but O'Brien's mind is so in tune with the horses he works with that he achieves tremendous satisfaction from being so closely involved. It's not just in the yard that he is near to them. He will often fly in the same plane when his horses travel to races overseas, and in the days when he had runners at Cheltenham he would fly there and back by helicopter so that he was at Ballydoyle for the gallops in the morning and for evening stables. When he has runners at big meetings in the summer, he will often ask the staff to come in early so that important gallops take place before he leaves for the races.

David Walsh of the *Sunday Times* spent several hours at Ballydoyle shortly after O'Brien's 2005 Newmarket Guineas double. One of the things that struck him most was what happened when the trainer's elder son, Joseph, rode his pony out of one of the stables. As it came through the door, the pony shot forward and 'spooked' at some unaccustomed sight. O'Brien quietly explained to his son that the pony had given himself a fright. He told the boy to take the animal back into the stable and come out a second time. But the pony had to walk out slowly and, once at the door, he was brought to a halt and allowed to look right and left before proceeding. This time the pony was not frightened and came out like a lamb. It might sound common sense, but most people connected with horses would not give it a thought. They would simply make sure that they sat tight to avoid being unseated by any spooking.

Clearly O'Brien would have no trouble obtaining a first were he to take a degree in equine psychology, if only he was able to put his innate knowledge into words. Sadly, and unfortunately for those aspiring to follow in his footsteps, he is not. However, the little that he does have to say is as informative as it is fascinating. Take this nugget on helping horses cope with defeat, for example:

> Horses know when they have won and, when Hawk Wing was beaten by Rock Of Gibraltar in the 2002 2,000 Guineas, the lads made a fuss of him so that both horses went home thinking they had won. If you were competing in something and you got beaten, you would get depressed if you were left alone afterwards. It's the same with horses. Also when you are racing two-year-olds the big thing is education and, if they get beaten first time out, you have to forgive them.

Vincent O'Brien was also a great believer in equine psychology. When he was buying yearlings, he would stand for minutes on end staring at their heads and eyes, trying to delve into their minds. In many ways comparisons between him and his successor are inevitable and only their records, when the latest O'Brien eventually decides to call it a day, will enable racing historians to say who was the better trainer.

Aidan O'Brien will probably end up with more big race winners on the Flat than Vincent O'Brien. No trainer has ever produced so many top-class horses, or won as many of the best races in so short a time, and he has already equalled Vincent's feat of winning three consecutive Champion Hurdles. Unless he changes direction once more, he will not match Vincent's four Cheltenham Gold Cups or win three successive Grand Nationals. However, he may well earn the right to dispute his predecessor's claim to be regarded as the greatest trainer of all time.

BIGGEST RACES WON

1995
Galway Plate	Life Of A Lord

1996
Royal & SunAlliance Novices' Hurdle	Urubande
Whitbread Gold Cup	Life Of A Lord
Galway Plate	Life Of A Lord
National Stakes	Desert King

1997
Royal & SunAlliance Novices' Hurdle	Istabraq
Irish 2,000 Guineas	Desert King
Irish 1,000 Guineas	Classic Park
Irish Derby	Desert King
Galway Hurdle	Toast The Spreece
National Stakes	King Of Kings
Racing Post Trophy	Saratoga Springs
Grand Criterium	Second Empire

1998
Champion Hurdle	Istabraq
2,000 Guineas	King Of Kings

Oaks	Shahtoush
Phoenix Stakes	Lavery
Prix Morny	Orpen
Fillies Mile	Sunspangled

1999

Champion Hurdle	Istabraq
Irish 2,000 Guineas	Saffron Walden
July Cup	Stravinsky
Phoenix Stakes	Fasliyev
Nunthorpe Stakes	Stravinsky
Prix Morny	Fasliyev
Racing Post Trophy	Aristotle
Prix de la Salamandre	Giant's Causeway
Grand Criterium	Ciro

2000

Champion Hurdle	Istabraq
Prix Lupin	Ciro
St James's Palace Stakes	Giant's Causeway
Coral-Eclipse Stakes	Giant's Causeway
Sussex Stakes	Giant's Causeway
Phoenix Stakes	Minardi
Juddmonte International	Giant's Causeway
Moyglare Stud Stakes	Sequoyah
National Stakes	Beckett
Irish Champion Stakes	Giant's Causeway
Middle Park Stakes	Minardi
Secretariat Stakes	Ciro

2001

| French 1,000 Guineas | Rose Gypsy |
| Irish 1,000 Guineas | Imagine |

Irish 2,000 Guineas	Black Minnaloushe
Oaks	Imagine
Derby	Galileo
St James's Palace Stakes	Black Minnaloushe
Irish Derby	Galileo
July Cup	Mozart
King George VI and Queen Elizabeth Stakes	Galileo
Prix Maurice de Gheest	King Charlemagne
Phoenix Stakes	Johannesburg
Prix Morny	Johannesburg
Nunthorpe Stakes	Mozart
Moyglare Stud Stakes	Quarter Moon
St Leger	Milan
National Stakes	Hawk Wing
Middle Park Stakes	Johannesburg
Dewhurst Stakes	Rock Of Gibraltar
Grand Criterium	Rock Of Gibraltar
Racing Post Trophy	High Chaparral
Gran Criterium	Sholokhov
Criterium de Saint-Cloud	Ballingarry
Breeders' Cup Juvenile	Johannesburg

2002

2,000 Guineas	Rock Of Gibraltar
French 2,000 Guineas	Landseer
Irish 2,000 Guineas	Rock Of Gibraltar
Derby	High Chaparral
St James's Palace Stakes	Rock Of Gibraltar
Coronation Stakes	Sophisticat
Irish Derby	High Chaparral
Phoenix Stakes	Spartacus
Coral-Eclipse Stakes	Hawk Wing
Sussex Stakes	Rock Of Gibraltar

Prix du Moulin   Rock Of Gibraltar
Grand Criterium   Hold That Tiger
Racing Post Trophy   Brian Boru
Criterium de Saint-Cloud   Alberto Giacometti
Gran Premio del Jockey Club   Black Sam Bellamy
Gran Criterium   Spartacus
Canadian International   Ballingarry
Shadwell Keeneland Turf Mile   Landseer
Breeders' Cup Turf   High Chaparral

2003

Lockinge Stakes   Hawk Wing
Tattersalls Gold Cup   Black Sam Bellamy
Irish 1,000 Guineas   Yesterday
Phoenix Stakes   One Cool Cat
Moyglare Stud Stakes   Necklace
Irish Champion Stakes   High Chaparral
St Leger   Brian Boru
National Stakes   One Cool Cat
Breeders' Cup Turf   High Chaparral

2004

Tattersalls Gold Cup   Powerscourt
Middle Park Stakes   Ad Valorem
Prix Jean-Luc Lagardère   Oratorio

2005

2,000 Guineas   Footstepsinthesand
1,000 Guineas   Virginia Waters
Coronation Cup   Yeats
Coral-Eclipse Stakes   Oratorio
Grand Prix de Paris   Scorpion
Phoenix Stakes   George Washington

Arlington Million	Powerscourt
Moyglare Stud Stakes	Rumplestiltskin
Irish Champion	Oratorio
St Leger	Scorpion
National Stakes	George Washington
Prix Marcel Boussac	Rumplestiltskin
Prix Jean-Luc Lagardère	Horatio Nelson

2006

2,000 Guineas	George Washington
French 2,000 Guineas	Aussie Rules
Oaks	Alexandrova
Queen Anne Stakes	Ad Valorem
Ascot Gold Cup	Yeats
Irish Derby	Dylan Thomas
Irish Oaks	Alexandrova
Phoenix Stakes	Holy Roman Emperor
Yorkshire Oaks	Alexandrova
Irish Champion Stakes	Dylan Thomas
Queen Elizabeth II Stakes	George Washington
Prix Jean-Luc Lagardère	Holy Roman Emperor
Criterium International	Mount Nelson
Shadwell Keeneland Turf Mile	Aussie Rules

2007

Prix Ganay	Dylan Thomas
French 2,000 Guineas	Astronomer Royal
Coronation Cup	Scorpion
St James's Palace Stakes	Excellent Art
Ascot Gold Cup	Yeats
Pretty Polly Stakes	Peeping Fawn
Irish Derby	Soldier Of Fortune
Irish Oaks	Peeping Fawn
King George VI and Queen Elizabeth Stakes	Dylan Thomas

2

EDWARD O'GRADY

Early in his training career, Edward O'Grady bestrode the heady atmosphere of the Cheltenham Festival like a colossus. Seldom did he fail to reward his legion of followers with at least one winner, and on many occasions his horses were the main reason why Irish punters returned home with money in their pockets. His reputation was further boosted by his role in one of the most famous betting coups in the long history of racing. Yet, astonishingly, he turned his back on the game with which he had made his mark to take on the big battalions on the Flat. It might be putting it too strongly to say he was a failure, but his achievements were small beer by comparison with what he had won under National Hunt rules. He made it back to the top over jumps to re-establish himself as one of the most successful Irish trainers of his era, but only after a tremendous struggle.

Edward O'Grady was bred for success in racing. His father, Willie, was twice Ireland's champion jockey, Flat and jumps combined, with seventy-four winners in 1934 and fifty-four the following year. His big race wins included the Galway Plate and the Grand Sefton – the latter contested over the Grand National fences – on a mare called Heartbreak Hill. He started training in 1940 and seven years later bought the County Tipperary yard at Ballynonty (between Littleton and Fethard) which his son was to inherit. In 1948, having ridden in the race eleven times without success, Willie ended his Irish National jinx with Hamstar, and he won it again with Icy Calm in 1951. At Cheltenham he was successful with Solfen in the Spa Hurdle and Broadway Novices' Chase, and with Kinloch Brae in the Cathcart Chase.

Willie's wife, Mary, was the sister of P.P. (Pat) Hogan, a legendary figure in the hunter chase and point-to-point circuit, first as a rider and then as a trainer. Hogan was also a particularly good judge of a Flat horse and was instrumental in the purchase of both the 1973 Arc de Triomphe winner Rheingold, and Assert who won the French and Irish Derby nine years later.

The O'Gradys' only child never gave much thought to a career outside racing. Nor was he encouraged to do so. He was only thirteen when he rode his first point-to-point winner, at Templemore on his mother's birthday. Royal Moon, the successful horse, was owned and bred by Barney Naughton, who was to become the owner of O'Grady junior's first Cheltenham winner, Mr Midland.

Willie O'Grady was a tough character who thought nothing of sitting up playing cards through the night and then going off hunting the next morning. A number of his contemporaries lived life in much the same colourful style, to the bemusement of modern-day trainers who feel they need all the sleep they can get and who well know that their owners would desert them if they adopted a similar approach to life.

Edward was packed off to veterinary college in Ballsbridge in Dublin when he left school. He would have preferred to have gone straight into the yard but his father bluntly told him, 'This place is not big enough for both of us. You'll have to go.'

Edward's ambitions as an amateur rider were also limited by his father's strongly held views. 'He believed that people who were paying good money to have their horses trained deserved something better than an unfit amateur who was normally away at school or college,' relates his son, who had barely fifty rides in his career and managed ten winners, including point-to-points.

In the summer of 1971 O'Grady junior received a phone call at the veterinary college to say that his father was dying. He had pneumonia and complications had set in. It was in the middle of exams, but Edward dropped everything to return home and keep the business going.

Willie O'Grady made a brief recovery but died early the following year. His hard-living lifestyle had taken its toll. He was only fifty-nine. His son was just twenty-two and needed another year to complete his qualifications. He hardly gave this a thought, but it was not long before he had cause to doubt the wisdom of turning his back on veterinary college.

He had his first winner almost immediately and a string of others quickly followed – 'I thought this signified that the training game had suddenly become easy,' he recalls – but among the horses at Ballynonty was a mare belonging to himself. He sent her away to be foaled and was horrified when he went to see her three days after the birth. She had become so thin that at first he did not recognise her. He brought her home and stabled both her and the foal in the yard with the eighteen racehorses he had taken over from his father. Four days later, one of them went down with a temperature of 103 degrees which rose rapidly to a near-fatal 106. The foal died at ten days old, and some of the racehorses followed suit. Those that survived went out to grass, the majority so badly affected that they never raced again.

The experts brought in by O'Grady diagnosed rhinopneumonitis, better known as virus abortion. None of them rubbed salt into the young trainer's wounds by saying that, if he had stayed at veterinary college, he would have known enough to at least suspect the disease and not make the disastrous mistake of allowing his racehorses to come into contact with an obviously sickening mare. But O'Grady was all too conscious of the gap in his education. 'You would have thought that I should have been more aware,' he muses now, the pain etched in the lines of his face as if it had all happened yesterday, 'but this was the first time we had ever had an outbreak of this type, and virus abortion was never even spoken of to me.'

O'Grady was young to start training. Three weeks before his father died, Edward had married Judy Mullins, a lively and vivacious girl whose ability to mix with people helped to resurrect her husband's career. After returning from a belated honeymoon, she and Edward set about filling the empty yard, her husband with one of his late father's maxims still ringing in his ears. 'Boy,' Willie had shouted at his son one day, 'you were not born with a silver spoon in your mouth. Go out and bloody work.' The young couple did not miss 'a cat or dog fight throughout the summer', as O'Grady recalls, and by the autumn there were twenty new horses in the yard.

It was not long before the winners began to flow once more and O'Grady felt sufficiently confident of continued success to take out a large loan in order to build a house for his mother across the road from the family home. But not for him the burden of a twenty-five-year mortgage and crippling monthly repayments. He resolved to pay off the lot with the sale of a horse called Stone Thrower. The gelding was six years old and had been slow to reach the racecourse, having reacted badly when given an injection.

O'Grady, who was still taking the occasional mount as an amateur claiming 7lb, rode Stone Thrower to finish sixth in a big field on his debut in a bumper at Leopardstown in April 1973. He knew the horse would come on sufficiently to be sure to win next time out and Tom Cooper, boss of the BBA (Ireland) bloodstock agency, approached him to ask if he had anything suitable for the Lambourn-based trainer Richard Head. O'Grady told him all about Stone Thrower and the price he wanted for a horse of considerable potential. It was a lot of money, but Cooper agreed to pay it, provided the gelding won on his next start.

This was in another bumper, at the Killarney May meeting, and O'Grady gave the ride to Mouse Morris, who was beginning to make a name for himself as an amateur. Stone Thrower was heavily backed and started favourite at even money. His trainer also rode in the race, but on a 20-1 no-hoper called No End, and his motives were entirely dishonourable. 'I naïvely had the idea that, if anything looked like getting close to Stone Thrower, I would run him off the course at the bottom bend.' He now acknowledges that he did not have the ability to execute such a manoeuvre against riders of the calibre of Ted Walsh, John Fowler, Michael Furlong and John Kiely, let alone do so sufficiently skilfully to avoid the attentions of the stewards.

Halfway up the straight, No End was still in mid-division and his rider stood up in the stirrups to make sure that the leader was in fact the favourite. When he saw Stone Thrower heading for the line three lengths clear, he cheered loudly and waved his whip in triumph. Returning to unsaddle, O'Grady, still grinning broadly, was met by No End's owner, Padge McCrea, demanding to know what the hell was going on. Halfway through a bottle of champagne in the bar, McCrea began to see the funny side, O'Grady repeatedly telling him 'I was riding for the house.'

Other winners landed more conventional gambles and O'Grady was an obvious candidate for the big-punting ambitions of Tony Murphy, a colourful Corkman who drove a silver Rolls-Royce, and who on Easter Monday 1974 had failed to bring off a spectacular off-course coup in Britain involving a non-runner. He resolved to try again at the August Bank Holiday meeting at Cartmel when the Cumbria course staged the most insignificant of that day's many race meetings. Cartmel was chosen because the course had no 'blower', the telephone link used by bookmakers to relay off-course bets back to the course in order to compress the starting prices. These are the prices at which such bets are settled, and are based on the average price quoted by the racecourse bookmakers for each horse at the moment the race starts.

Murphy's plan was to include a horse that was certain to win in a treble involving two no-hopers that would be withdrawn from their respective races, both at other meetings. All three would come from a little-known stable, but in fact the 'job' horse would be trained by an accomplished professional, in this case O'Grady.

The official trainer was to be Tony Collins, a stockbroker who trained a small string of his own horses as a sideline in Scotland, not far from the famous Troon golf course. Murphy's choice for the surefire winner was a four-year-old named Gay Future, who had won for Johnny Harrington (later to marry trainer Jessica) at Thurles in the spring of 1974. O'Grady bought the horse to pass on to Collins, but kept him in his own yard to prepare him for the race.

However, when Gay Future arrived at Cartmel he was officially trained by Collins, as were two other horses running that day, Opera Cloak at Southwell and Ankerwyke at Plumpton. These were the no-hopers that Murphy and his cohorts had included in the treble bets they placed at betting shops all over London. The bookmakers took little notice because the stakes were small, assuming in addition that anybody who backed a treble with two horses that patently had no chance did not know what they were doing. It was quite late in the afternoon when the bookies realised that Opera Cloak and Ankerwyke were not going to run. The former's race was due off at 4.15 p.m. and Ankerwyke's half an hour later. Gay Future's race, the Ulverston Novices' Hurdle, was at 4.20 p.m. Since this horse was the only one of the three actually running, the entire stake went on him.

Murphy arranged for other horses in the Cartmel race to be backed in order to push out Gay Future's starting price. Furthermore, soap flakes were rubbed on to the horse's neck and flanks before he went into the parade ring to make it look as if he was sweating himself into a bag of nerves. Timmy Jones, the amateur who had ridden Gay Future when he won at Thurles, again had the mount, but he went down to the start with his stirrups long so that he looked incompetent. Murphy and most of his fellow backers were still in London when Gay Future romped home fifteen lengths clear at 10-1.

The London bookmakers immediately smelled a rat, and most of them refused to pay out. The Jockey Club made inquiries and found that neither Opera Cloak nor Ankerwyke had ever left Troon. Murphy had arranged with Collins that both horses would travel to their respective racecourses: one horse would then be withdrawn because the horsebox had broken down en route to the racecourse, and a similar concocted excuse would be put forward for the other one. However, Collins, unbeknownst to Murphy, simply decided to leave the horses in their stables. He later complained that he had not been told that Murphy and his friends were going to include the two non-runners in a treble. His own bets were simply on Gay Future.

Murphy, who soon returned to Cork, was arrested when he arrived at Cheltenham the following March. So too were some of the others involved in the coup, including O'Grady. They were driven to the police station in the Cumbrian town of Kendal and charged with conspiracy to defraud. Collins was arrested in Troon. However, the charges were later dropped against everyone except Murphy and Collins. Both escaped with a £1,000 fine plus £500 costs. The Jockey Club banned the pair from all British racecourses for ten years.

The failed coup was made into a seventy-five-minute film called *Murphy's Stroke*, starring Pierce Brosnan. Early in 2006 TG4, the Irish-language television station, showed a follow-up in the form of a short documentary. O'Grady claims not to have seen the latter programme, and the Gay Future affair is an episode in his career that he refuses to discuss. 'I have never spoken much about it,' he insists in the tone he uses when he is determined to put a stop to further questions.

O'Grady might now view the coup as an embarrassment, but at the time it added considerably to his reputation as a trainer with a talent for preparing a horse for the big day, when owners could put their money down with confidence. He had considerable success at Cheltenham and at the big Irish festival in Galway. Not many trainers are able to do both, not least because Galway takes place at the height of the summer when most of the best jumpers are only just coming back from their holidays out at grass.

In 1978 O'Grady won the Galway Plate with Shining Hope, and the following year he took both the famous steeplechase and the Galway Hurdle with Hindhope and Hard Tarquin. He also prepared Rugged Lucy to win the Galway Plate in 1981. However, it was at the Cheltenham Festival that he excelled. He had his first winner there with Mr Midland, in Barney Naughton's colours, in the National Hunt Chase, little more than two years after he had started training, and at only one meeting between 1976 and 1984 did he not walk in triumph into the most hallowed winner's enclosure in jump racing, the deafening cheers of Irish racegoers accompanying his every step.

O'Grady did this at a time when Irish-trained Cheltenham winners were measured, not in the nine or ten of recent years, but in numbers often only half that figure. Nor is it entirely coincidental that Ireland's success at the greatest National Hunt meeting in the world dried up to a trickle when O'Grady elected to move into Flat racing. Undoubtedly the best of his Cheltenham winners was Golden Cygnet, many respected professionals' idea of the best hurdler of all time. He wasn't much to look at, his unprepossessing appearance being one of the main reasons why his trainer was able to pick him up for only 980 guineas at Goffs bloodstock sales as an unbroken three-year-old. Golden Cygnet had what appeared like foal hair on him and O'Grady describes his appearance as 'like a horse who had come from a very poor hotel, although he hadn't. That was simply the nature of the beast.'

Golden Cygnet was bought for Ray Rooney, who has an insurance agency in Galway, plays a big part in the Galway Festival meeting and was later senior steward of the Turf Club. Rooney took in a few friends as partners in the horse, but O'Grady's initial progress reports were disturbing. 'He proved next to impossible to break. It wasn't so much that he was badly behaved as that he used to plant everybody and was almost unrideable as a result. When we eventually got him going, he galloped with his head between his knees to such an extent that he would hit them with his teeth. This made the knees sore and swollen.'

O'Grady, racking his brains for a solution, recalled seeing the strange leather contraptions worn by showjumpers in their warm-up work and drove to the Dublin Horse Show to talk to the top riders. Among those he consulted was Harvey Smith, and he returned home with the design for a leather cover for Golden Cygnet's knees. No sooner did the horse start wearing the covers than he changed his action so that his teeth no longer came into contact with his legs.

Golden Cygnet showed ability on the Flat, so much so that he was backed from 20-1 to 7-2 for the 1977 Leopardstown November Handicap. On this occasion, as in several other races, he ran below expectations. However, it was a different story when he was put over hurdles and by the time it came to the 1978 Supreme Novices' Hurdle, his reputation was so exalted that he started at 5-4 on.

Punters ignored the bay gelding's sparely made frame, while horse-flesh connoisseurs gathered around the parade ring preferred to comment on his intelligent expression and his unusual face markings – below the star on his forehead was a white blaze in the form of an inverted V. By the time the field reached the second last flight, Golden Cygnet was pulling double over his rivals. As soon as his rider let him go, he stormed clear. He flew the last and strode up the final hill like a champion to win by the staggering margin of fifteen lengths.

After a bloodless win at Fairyhouse, he was sent to Ayr for the Scottish Champion Hurdle. This was a handicap and the British handicapper thought so much of Golden Cygnet that he gave the horse 11st 13lb, only 1lb less than that year's Champion Hurdle runner-up, Sea Pigeon, and 5lb more than Night Nurse who had won the Champion Hurdle in each of the two previous seasons. Golden Cygnet started joint favourite with Sea Pigeon and was going best of all when he fell heavily at the final flight. O'Grady did not at first realise that the horse was seriously hurt.

What happened when I went to see him in the racecourse stables was extraordinary. He came up to me and rubbed the left side of his head against my shoulder. He then took half a step back and rubbed the right side of his head against me. He did this in a slightly loving way as if to say 'Look, I've got something wrong with me.' I decided it was probably a vertebra in his neck and, as we had such a wonderful opinion of him and because my own horsebox was at the racecourse, we drove him straight to the Royal Dick veterinary hospital in Edinburgh.

I flew home that evening and the vets in Edinburgh reported to me the following morning that he'd had a good night. On Monday I went to the evening meeting in Roscommon. I came home a bit tired and was sitting down having a boiled egg when the phone rang. They told me he had had a brain haemorrhage and they had put him down.

When O'Grady talks about Golden Cygnet, he repeatedly uses the words 'extraordinary horse'. One of the reasons is the way the gelding raced. 'He was the opposite to almost every other horse. They are invariably keen at the start and pooped at the finish, but with Golden Cygnet the most unimpressive part of his races came at the beginning. The farther he went, the better he got, and he would finish as fresh as a horse going down to the start.'

At the end of that season Timeform gave Golden Cygnet a rating of 176. The horse was still only a novice, but that assessment puts him ahead of many winners of the Champion Hurdle. Night Nurse was the best of them all, or at least the best since Timeform's ratings began in 1962; he was rated 182 at the end of the 1976/77 season, though past his best by the time Golden Cygnet took him on that day at Ayr. But Sea Pigeon later earned a rating of 175; the performance of O'Grady's horse against two such rivals was remarkable and fully warranted all the superlatives heaped on him. 'It's difficult to say exactly how good he was,' his trainer concedes. 'He was certainly the best I ever had and I would like to think that he was the best I saw over hurdles. I could be biased, but the fact that he had Night Nurse and Sea Pigeon, two of the best hurdlers ever, stone cold going to the last is my yardstick.'

Golden Cygnet was ridden in all his hurdles races by Niall 'Boots' Madden, whose son 'Slippers' won the 2006 Grand National on Numbersixvalverde. Madden senior is even more emphatic than O'Grady: 'He was a freak. Early in a race you would be pushing him along, yet when you said it was time to go, he would rev up underneath you, and he had some gears for a National Hunt horse. He was the best hurdler ever.'

O'Grady was understandably upset at the news of Golden Cygnet's death, but not so distraught as he might have been. 'Being so young, I fully expected that another every bit as good would come along and I simply didn't realise that a horse of his ability would prove to be quite so rare.'

Edward O'Grady became far more grief-stricken as he grew older. All trainers find the death of a good horse hard to take, but few are as badly affected as O'Grady. He can retreat into a shell and refuse to talk about the horse.

A lot of thought goes into training and I get pretty fond of my horses. With a good one I form a unison, and there is not a horse born who is uncomplicated. They are like children to begin with and invariably there proves to be an Achilles heel somewhere along the line, just as with people. Because of the unison I form with the good ones, I try to plan their whole career and I avoid more pots than I attack as I'm taking the long road. I cosset them and when something awful happens I feel 'I've done everything for you and you've let me down.' I also ask 'Have I let you down? Have I done something I shouldn't? Should I have run you in that race?'

O'Grady had been training for less than ten years when he began to hanker after the bigger rewards to be had on the Flat. He eyed the equine battalion at Ballydoyle barely twelve miles away, where horses were being turned into stallions worth millions, and he knew that he wanted more out of life than jump racing could offer. Financially at least, it did not offer anything like enough for the trainer or his clients.

> By the end of the 1970s interest rates had gone up to twenty per cent. I was training for a lot of strong farmers and, in those days, the stronger they were, the more debt they had. Land had gone up to nearly £5,000 an acre but none of them ever imagined that interest rates were going to go so high, or that farming could slump. They found it difficult to pay their bills and, like any normal businessmen, they decided that something had to go. That was the racehorse. Therefore it seemed a commercially correct decision for me to find clients who were more liquid, and these people were more attracted to the Flat.

O'Grady joined forces with BBA (Ireland) director Adrian Nicoll to put syndicates together in order to buy yearlings that could show a profit if trained successfully and then resold. Nicoll had the contacts to place horses that had won, or were clearly about to do so, with buyers around the globe, and O'Grady had the ability to bring out the best in the horses.

The partnership was a commercial success for both men, and O'Grady was also able to attract patronage from wealthy owners like Robert Sangster and Lady Clague. However, few of the horses he was sent were anywhere near good enough to compete at the top level, let alone take on the likes of Vincent O'Brien. As a result, success in big races eluded O'Grady, and so did the publicity he needed to attract top horses. He still trained a few jumpers, but their standard was on the decline. Traditional National Hunt owners, seeing his expansion into the Flat, concluded that he no longer had the same interest in jumping and so they went to other trainers. O'Grady's numbers began to decline and, on the often vicious but exceedingly influential racecourse grapevine, word spread that O'Grady was on a downward spiral.

The trainer was even more aware than the rumour-mongers that he needed to pull something out of the bag. His initial satisfaction at being better off had begun to wane, particularly when he saw how much the prize money was being increased for hurdle and steeplechase races.

> It was coming up to the sort of level I wished it had been earlier in my career. Also, while I was financially successful as a Flat trainer, I was a small minnow in a very big pool. As a National Hunt trainer I felt I could be a bigger fish in a smaller pond, and that was something I might prefer. In any case I never had more than about twenty-five Flat horses. I wasn't a trainer that breeders would send many horses to, and they are the backbone of any Flat stable.

But O'Grady found it hard to attract National Hunt owners. Many of those who had supported him in his pre-Flat days had died, dropped out or moved to other yards, and for some there was a suspicion that he might have lost his touch. Good horses proved equally hard to come by and not until 1994 (ten years after Northern Game's success in the Triumph Hurdle) was he able to put his name back on the Cheltenham score sheet. When he did so, with Time For A Run and Mucklemeg, it seemed appropriate that both horses should be owned by J.P. McManus, because the former bookmaker was one of the few who had kept jumpers with O'Grady throughout the Flat years.

McManus's association with O'Grady began with Jack Of Trumps in 1977 and it has continued unbroken ever since. McManus was initially attracted by the trainer's ability to train a horse on which he (McManus) could have a sizeable punt, and he intended to have a big bet on Time For A Run in the 1994 Coral Cup. O'Grady, beginning to despair of returning to the hallowed Cheltenham winner's enclosure after the opening-day defeats of fancied horses, famously instructed Charlie Swan to 'ride with balls of steel'. Unfortunately for McManus, the bookies would offer him only 8-1 when the horse started at 11-1, and he allowed his winner to go unbacked.

However, Time For A Run and Mucklemeg ensured that O'Grady was back with a bang, and five further Cheltenham Festival winners have brought his total to eighteen; Vincent O'Brien and Tom Dreaper are the only Irish trainers to have done better. O'Grady's tally far exceeds that of any of his present rivals in Ireland, thus confirming his status as a truly outstanding jumping trainer.

O'Grady firmly believes that buying the right horse is a key ingredient, perhaps the most important one of all.

> If you were to walk through the Garden of Eden, you would see many apples before you found the one you really wanted to pick. It's then a case of whether you have faith in that apple or whether you decide you should go for something else.
>
> Also a lot of thought goes into training horses. The year that Time For A Run won the Coral Cup, we'd had two beaten favourites on the first day of the meeting in Sound Man and Gimme Five. I thought I had done everything right, but what I hadn't done was give Charlie Swan any instructions. I didn't think they were necessary but, as it turned out, they were. That was why I repeatedly stressed to him that he was to ride Time For A Run the way he did.

O'Grady can be a formidable man to cross, as some in the press have found to their cost. Many years ago he took exception to a series of letters in *The Irish Field* about a horse of his that had been the subject of a gamble. O'Grady was as annoyed with the newspaper as he was with the letter writers – he felt that the subject should have been dropped after a week – and when driving from the airport into Dublin one day he spotted the paper's editor, Valentine Lamb, standing at a bus stop. Lamb was barely inside the car when the haranguing began, and they travelled much of the way into the city before O'Grady let up.

On another occasion a journalist questioned the resolution of Ventana Canyon, O'Grady's winner of the 1996 Arkle Trophy. When the horse won at Punchestown the following month, the trainer immediately started shouting for the hack to come forward.

There have been changes in the Ballynonty household in recent years, and many were astonished when they heard that Edward and Judy O'Grady had split up. Judy had always appeared to be close to her husband, as well as an essential part of the team. The new Mrs O'Grady first appeared on the racing scene as the owner of Sheltering when the gelding won on his racecourse debut at Limerick in March 1999. At least that is the first time most racegoers became aware of Maria Anderton – and to them she was simply a tall, fair-haired woman whose colours were carried to victory by a horse of considerable promise. She is now the mother of O'Grady's two young children. His and Judy's three have long since grown up and left home.

Maria plays an integral role in the training set-up and her husband speaks of his 'young family' with both pride and satisfaction. 'I now want to continue doing what I am doing, which is enjoying a very good standard of living and having a way of life that I like with people that I like,' he adds, a smile of contentment on his face. 'If I can also improve the quality of the horses, or the way I train them, I am very ambitious to do so.'

He restricts himself to seventy horses, because more might bring staffing problems, and more horses would mean more bad ones. 'If you can differentiate the wheat from the chaff, you will end up with less bad horses and you are not having to employ more men, build more gallops or buy more corn.'

The government's enormous annual cash injection into prize money has meant that O'Grady is now able to reap the sort of rewards that took him on that disappointing detour into Flat racing.

For twenty-eight years I lost money on the training and I was dependent on buying, selling and gambling. The whole ethos has changed thanks to Denis Brosnan [chairman of Horse Racing Ireland]. Ministers Charlie McCreevy and Joe Walsh put the package together but there is no doubt in my mind that Denis was the one in the driving seat, and without him we would not have got the same result.

O'Grady shakes his head in mock despair as he talks about the way some of his rivals complain about their situation. 'There are an awful lot of trainers who grumble but they just don't realise what it was like running for £500 and training for £8 a week, and then you sometimes couldn't get paid. God Almighty!'

BIGGEST RACES WON

1974
National Hunt Chase   Mr Midland

1976
Kim Muir Chase   Prolan

1977
Cathcart Chase   Rusty Tears

1978
Supreme Novices' Hurdle   Golden Cygnet
Stayers' Hurdle   Flame Gun
Galway Plate   Shining Hope

1979

Galway Plate	Hindhope
Galway Hurdle	Hard Tarquin

1980

SunAlliance Novices' Hurdle	Drumlargan
Stayers' Hurdle	Mountrivers

1981

County Hurdle	Staplestown
Galway Plate	Rugged Lucy

1982

SunAlliance Novices' Hurdle	Mister Donovan

1983

National Hunt Chase	Bit Of A Skite
Irish Grand National	Bit Of A Skite
Whitbread Gold Cup	Drumlargan

1984

Triumph Hurdle	Northern Game

1994

Coral Cup	Time For A Run
Champion Bumper	Mucklemeg

1995

Tingle Creek Chase	Sound Man

1996

Arkle Trophy	Ventana Canyon
National Hunt Chase	Loving Around

Tingle Creek Chase   Sound Man

2002
AIG Europe Champion Hurdle   Ned Kelly
Champion Bumper   Pizarro

2003
Supreme Novices' Hurdle   Back In Front

2006
Coral Cup   Sky's The Limit

3

WILLIE MULLINS

Aintree, 9 April 2005. Hedgehunter, the 7-1 favourite for the Grand National, is comfortably clear as he lands over the final fence. Ruby Walsh, determined not to let his mount falter on the long run-in, hardly moves a muscle until he reaches the famous elbow. The crowd roars as the favourite romps home fourteen lengths clear. Up in the stands Paddy Mullins, recently retired after training for half a century, has his hand repeatedly shaken and says that simply being at the Liverpool course to witness this is better than any of his own achievements. The runaway Grand National winner is trained by his son.

Willie Mullins, an outstanding amateur rider, has done even better as a trainer. In addition to winning the world's greatest steeplechase, he has a tremendous record at the Cheltenham Festival, particularly in the Champion Bumper. He has also played a prominent role on the political side of racing: his lengthy period as chairman of the Irish Racehorse Trainers' Association coincided with the Turf Club handing over many of its powers in return for huge state funding for racing.

Paddy Mullins had been training for less than four years when Willie was born on 15 September 1956. His sister, Sandra, was less than a year old. Three more brothers were to follow: George (1959), Tony (1962) and Tom (1964). Paddy and his wife Maureen trained at

Doninga House on the outskirts of Goresbridge in County Kilkenny. In those days they operated on a very small scale. The outside staff initially consisted of only one stable lad and in the first five years the yard had only a handful of winners.

Mullins senior would have moved into the big time much earlier than he did had he found an owner to hold on to Nicolaus Silver. When neighbouring trainer Dan Kirwan died in 1960, the grey was one of a number of horses that moved to Doninga, but he was sold at Goffs that November for 2,600 guineas and bought by Worcestershire trainer Fred Rimell. Mullins recalls:

> I thought it was a very small price, but I had no owner to buy him. However Paddy Sleator was heard to remark that the horse would be nearer his value if you took a nought off the end. Little more than four months later he won the Grand National. From the way Fred spoke after the race, you would think that he had foaled the horse himself and trained him ever since. I could never bear Fred after that!

Willie was too young to appreciate the significance of what might have been, although he was already riding ponies. He was seventeen when he had his first ride on the racecourse. He came home for the weekend from his boarding school in Roscrea to be told by his father that he had taken out an amateur rider's licence for him and that he had a mount at Fairyhouse the following day. However, it was nine months before he rode a winner – Silver Road at Tramore. The horse was owned by Ed Green, a Florida businessman, who came to Ireland the following summer partly to see Silver Road race. Mullins, father and son, were optimistic that the gelding would win an amateur handicap hurdle at Bellewstown at the end of June. Silver Road started joint second favourite, but Green was disappointed to see his seven-year-old finish only third, five lengths behind a 20-1 shot. However, he went home with a story to enthral his friends for the rest of his days: the rank outsider, Yellow Sam, who had no form to recommend him, brought off in that race one of the most famous gambles of the last century.

The horse was owned by Barney Curley, who had trained for the priesthood only to turn his back on holy orders and become a professional gambler. He put Yellow Road in his wife's colours and sent him to be trained by ex-jockey Liam Brennan with a view to bringing off a coup. Having chosen the race at Bellewstown because the hilltop racecourse had only one telephone, Curley backed the horse to win almost £300,000 at starting price in betting shops all over Ireland, placing the bets in small amounts so as not to alarm the bookmakers. But when they tried to lay off part of the money with the course bookmakers and so reduce the starting price, they found the phone number perpetually engaged. Curley had a large power-fully built man on the other end, supposedly deep in conversation with a sick relative, while he himself watched proceedings from behind the bushes by the third last hurdle. Curley tried the same trick again at Downpatrick later the same year, but on that occasion his 25-1 shot was beaten a short head by the odds-on favourite.

Mullins was twenty-five when he rode his first Cheltenham winner, Hazy Dawn, in the 1982 National Hunt Chase. The mare was owned by country and western singer Roly Daniels, who had the huge crowds roaring for more when he sang 'Danny Boy' in the winner's enclosure. For the horse's rider, the exhilaration of victory was tinged with relief.

For the first half of the four miles I just hacked round, but I began to get into the race as we jumped the water for the last time. I couldn't believe how well she was travelling at the open ditch nearing the top of the hill but I said to myself 'I am just going to sit, and then jump home.' I led at the second last but, as I turned for home, I got the fright of my life. I looked up the straight and I couldn't see the last fence. I thought 'Oh my God, I've taken the wrong course.' I blinked, and there was the fence straight in front of me. I don't know exactly how it happened but it must have been the angle of the sun and the shadow from the stands. Whatever it was, I was mightily relieved as I jumped the fence and swept up the hill seven lengths in front.

For Paddy Mullins, who trained Hazy Dawn, this still ranks as his greatest Cheltenham moment, despite subsequent wins in the Champion Hurdle and the Gold Cup with Dawn Run. 'I still regard that Gold Cup victory as a bit of a disappointment,' he explains. 'She was a super mare, but to be asked to prepare a horse like her to win the race and be treated the way I was, sickened me.' He was referring to the decision of owner Charmian Hill to jock off son Tony Mullins after he was unseated from Dawn Run when the mare ran in a race over the same course two months earlier.

Willie also won the 1984 National Hunt Chase for his father on Macks Friendly. The previous year his handling of Atha Cliath in the Foxhunters at Aintree had earned him rave reviews in the press. He stuck like glue to the inside rail all the way round: in the sitting room of his home, there is a painting by Peter Curling of him jumping the Canal Turn, his boot scraping the paint of the rail. The ride was all the more remarkable because Mullins's usual tactic in races in Ireland was to give the outside to no one. He was often criticised by punters for forfeiting so much ground, but he reasoned: 'The going was normally so churned up by the time it came to the bumper that I had to go to the outside to get decent ground, and I am convinced the advantage of this more than made up for travelling a few extra lengths.'

By this stage, Willie's younger brother Tony was beginning to make his mark. He soon became stable jockey to his father, and was Ireland's champion jump jockey in 1984 and again in 1988/89. Willie envied the money Tony was making. As an amateur he was not, strictly speaking, allowed to earn anything, although it is accepted practice in Ireland for accomplished 'amateurs' to be paid a fee in cash for each ride, plus a percentage of prize money whenever they win a race (the Turf Club conveniently turns a blind eye to this breach of the rules). Willie put everything he had into trying to win the amateurs' championship, even hiring a private plane one Saturday late in 1984 so that he could ride at Clonmel and Fairyhouse in the same afternoon. His efforts appeared to have been in vain when Ted Walsh finished the year one winner in front of him, but one of Walsh's mounts later failed a dope test and was disqualified, so technically the pair shared the title. Mullins was to win it outright in 1985. Three further championships followed before he tied with Frances Crowley (the first woman to become champion amateur in Ireland) in 1995/96.

Willie was always too heavy to turn pro and, looking at his big frame, you would wonder how he was ever light enough to ride in races. By the time he reached the age of twenty-one, he envisaged becoming a trainer, but he saw little point in rushing into it while he was enjoying an exciting life riding in races. He toyed with the idea of going to America or Australia for a summer to gain experience but instead accepted an offer to join Jim Bolger's operation. He knew that the Coolcullen trainer was a hard taskmaster but there were a number of decent bumper horses in the yard, and Mullins thought he would be able to ride them in their races. In fact, he did not get that many mounts from his new boss, but what he did receive was a weekly wage.

It was the first time I really earned any money. At home, working for my father, I just got a few quid here and there. I spent just over a year at Jim's; it was totally different from working at home and it taught me a few things. One was that I wasn't cut out for working for somebody else. Maybe I'd spent too long at home and having things my own way. When the fire at Jim's stables happened in 1982, everybody became in miserable form and I didn't enjoy life there. I said to myself that, no matter how much money I was earning, it was no good if I wasn't enjoying things and so I left.

It was his marriage to Jackie that finally persuaded Willie Mullins to start training. The daughter of a doctor in Essex, she already had a law degree when she travelled to Ireland to buy an eventer, and it was then that she met her future husband. Her uncle, Jim Callaghan, was a doctor in Carlow and Paddy Mullins was one of his patients. When he began to make money as a trainer, Mullins senior had bought land at Closutton, just off the main road between Carlow and Kilkenny and not far from the Burgage Stud. He thought he would use the land for grazing and for keeping horses that were either not yet ready to go into training or that needed a rest. It was here that Willie started training at the beginning of 1988 while brother George used part of the same land for his horse transport and paper-bedding business.

There were twenty stables in the yard and a one-storey house at the end of it. Both have since been considerably extended, but the new inmate had only half a dozen horses when he started. Within eight months he had trained nine winners and increased the string to ten. The real breakthrough came when he won the 1995 Supreme Novices' Hurdle with Tourist Attraction.

It's hard to beat the feeling you get from your first Festival winner. Hazy Dawn had been special and Tourist Attraction was every bit as good. She started at 25-1 but her victory came as no surprise to us. Ventana Canyon started joint second favourite that day [he finished second] and Tourist Attraction had beaten him in a bumper at Punchestown the previous April. I felt that if Ventana Canyon was that much fancied, our mare had to have just as good a chance.

Success at Cheltenham always attracts owners, and Mullins's stable was beginning to take on some quality horses by the time Wither Or Which caused a minor sensation when scoring by twenty lengths on his debut at Leopardstown on New Year's Eve 1995. It was a huge margin and Mullins left few in any doubt about the esteem in which he held the horse. He was even more bullish in the build-up to Cheltenham, saying that this was the best horse he had ever ridden, including everything he had sat on in his father's yard, with the possible exception of Dawn Run – 'I did very little on her so she doesn't come into the equation.'

There was some surprise when the trainer insisted on keeping the mount himself. The Champion Bumper, added to the Cheltenham card in 1992 to increase Ireland's chances of success at a time when the visitors were going through a lean spell, had become established as a race that was invariably won by a professional jockey. Furthermore, Mullins was only six months away from his fortieth birthday. He declared that he was not worried about any of his professional opponents and pointed out that he had beaten most of them at one time or another. It was fighting talk but it intensified the weight of expectation. He admitted afterwards that, while he had felt no pressure before going out to ride either Hazy Dawn or Macks Friendly at Cheltenham, he did so on this occasion. Fortunately, it didn't affect his performance, and Mullins became one of a select few to have both ridden and trained the same horse to win at the Festival.

Twelve months later, though, he handed over the ride on Florida Pearl to Richard Dunwoody. This white-faced bay was to be the stable's principal flag-bearer for eight seasons, winning sixteen of his thirty-three starts, including nine Grade One races. He was owned by Violet O'Leary and her husband Archie, who comes from Cork, a notable rugby player in his youth who donned the Irish green jersey three times in 1952 and has since built up a successful insurance-broking business.

The O'Learys did not accompany Mullins when the trainer, scouting for talent, visited Tom Costello's horse farm at Newmarket-on-Fergus, County Clare in February 1996. Costello has hundreds of prospective jumpers, all for sale, while his four sons have similar but smaller farms nearby, and after inspecting some of Costello senior's stock, Mullins called at John Costello's place. It was here that he was struck by the way that a gelding by little-known sire Florida Son moved when walked and trotted for inspection: 'He covered an awful lot of ground and he was all power behind.' However, Costello told him that the four-year-old was not for sale, at least not yet. He added that, for the amount of money he wanted, the horse would have to prove to be as good as he (Costello) was convinced he was, and he could do that only by winning a race. It was powerful sales talk, but Mullins was so impressed with the horse that he agreed to wait until the gelding ran in a point-to-point at Lismore on 3 March. Apart from anything else, it would give him time to find a client.

O'Leary was one of four people who had told Mullins to let them know when he found a nice horse, and he was the first of the quartet to commit himself to accompanying the trainer on his return trip to Newmarket-on-Fergus. They struck a deal with Costello at IR£50,000, and if O'Leary ever had second thoughts, they were dispelled even before Florida Pearl romped home five lengths clear on his racecourse debut in the same Leopardstown bumper that Wither Or Which had won twelve months earlier. Word soon spread about how good the new Mullins horse was, both at home and when taken away for gallops, and before the Leopardstown race O'Leary was offered St£120,000 for him. He had no hesitation in turning it down. He had bought Florida Pearl in the hope that the gelding would develop into a top-class horse, not to make a quick profit.

On his second start, Florida Pearl won the Champion Bumper at Cheltenham, and the way he did it convinced his trainer that he should defy convention and forego a season over hurdles.

When Richard Dunwoody moved on him to take a position at the top of the hill, he absolutely zoomed up. Richard then took a pull, but when Florida Pearl was asked to go again he quickened once more. This showed he could act round Cheltenham and I decided there and then that he was a chaser, so why bother going hurdling with him? I also knew that, since he could act so well round Cheltenham, there was a huge race in him there, assuming all went well. Also he had already proved in that point-to-point at Lismore that he could jump fences.

Florida Pearl was so impressive in his first race over fences that some began calling him the next Arkle. He was not the first, and certainly not the last, to be dubbed with this doubtful epithet and, like all the others, he failed to live up to the almost impossible billing. But he proved to be a cracking good horse and he extended his unbeaten run to five when returning to Cheltenham to win the 1998 Royal & SunAlliance Chase. At Leopardstown the following February he won the first of four Hennessy Gold Cups and he started favourite for the Cheltenham Gold Cup. He finished third to See More Business and in the same race twelve months later was second to Looks Like Trouble. Maybe he might have gone even closer in 2001 – at the age of nine he was at his prime – but the meeting was lost to the foot and mouth outbreak that brought racing in Ireland to a halt and severely curtailed the programme in Britain.

In truth, Florida Pearl did not stay the final two and a half furlongs of the Gold Cup trip and he had such a high cruising speed that many in the media repeatedly told Mullins that he was running the horse in the wrong race. (Mullins bowed to their pressure in 2003 and aimed him at the Queen Mother Champion Chase instead, but Florida Pearl was simply not fast enough to take on the best two-milers and he finished unplaced.) Like many horses given star billing when they were young, Florida Pearl came in for criticism in the press almost every time he was beaten and, when he went for the King George VI Chase at Kempton on Boxing Day 2001, so much of the gloss had been knocked off him that Mullins could not find a rider. Ruby Walsh, the stable jockey, had never seemed to get on particularly well with the horse and said that he would prefer to ride at the big Leopardstown meeting. Paul Carberry, who had won many races on Florida Pearl, initially suggested that he might be available, but his agent rang Mullins to say that Carberry's commitments to Noel Meade meant that he could not take the ride.

I was surprised that neither jockey would change their arrangements to ride what was arguably the best chaser in the country in the best chase in England outside the Gold Cup. I simply couldn't understand their way of thinking. By that stage all the top jockeys in Britain had committed themselves either to other horses in the race or to different meetings. I picked out J.P. McNamara on the understanding that, if one of the top riders became available, he would take his place. J.P. was at home in Ireland for Christmas but he flew back to England to school the horse at Kempton on Christmas Eve.

One of the jockeys that Mullins had tried to book was Adrian Maguire, who was on his way to Wetherby on Boxing Day when he heard at 8.30 a.m. that the meeting had been called off. He was riding for Ferdy Murphy, who wanted him to divert to Market Rasen, but at 10 a.m. he received a call from his agent to say that Murphy had agreed that he could be released from his commitments to take the mount on Florida Pearl. Even then it was not plain sailing. Maguire was delayed by traffic on the M25 and reached Kempton only as the first race was about to begin. However, all went well once he was in the saddle. Maguire took it up with almost a circuit to run. His mount was able to dictate the pace from then on and, aided by some particularly fluent jumping, kept up the gallop to beat Best Mate by three-quarters of a length.

Mullins was thrilled:

Not having a jockey had made for a nerve-racking few days and winning the race after all that meant more to me than any of his previous wins, the two at Cheltenham included. He was lame early in the season and early the previous one, and as a result his preparation for the James Nicholson Champion Chase was curtailed each time.

Those two races were probably the ones that disappointed people most and I think were the main reason why he got so much flak. We then discovered that the lameness was due to a fractured splint bone which we treated with a few pricks of a pinfire. He was a marvellous horse and an absolute treasure to train.

O'Leary and his wife also owned By My Royal, who won the 2002 Hennessy Gold Cup at Newbury, beating the biggest field the race had seen for forty years. The eight-year-old was 9lb out of the handicap and started at 33-1. He took it up after jumping the final fence, but broke down so badly close to the line – before coming home by half a length – that it was thought he would never be able to race again. That was bad enough, but days later the routine dope test revealed traces of morphine in his system.

Mullins gets much of his feedstuffs from Connolly's Red Mills in Goresbridge. A batch had somehow become contaminated, although the morphine traces were so slight that they were not picked up by the firm's own testing procedures. Connolly's also supplied many other stables, in Britain as well as Ireland, and the faulty batch was responsible for positive tests on thirty-seven horses in Britain and nine in Ireland. The company paid the prize money to the owners and trainers of the disqualified horses, and took the Jockey Club to court in a bid to get the rules changed so that minute traces of morphine and other prohibited substances would not lead to automatic disqualification. The court case was fronted by Mullins, who shared Connolly's concerns, although it was the Goresbridge firm that picked up the tab for all the legal costs. The case dragged on for more than three years; including prize money paid out, it cost Connolly's an estimated 1 million euro. The High Court in Britain ruled against the firm, but the Jockey Club did make a partial amendment to the relevant rules. Joe Connolly, boss of his family's company, knew he had to fight the case almost regardless of cost, because a second outbreak of disqualifications could see him losing customers in droves, putting the company in danger of going under.

Mullins believes in an attacking policy with his best horses and he has twice won the French Champion Hurdle, the Grande Course de Haies at Auteuil in Paris. This was the race that his father had won with Dawn Run in 1984, with Tony Mullins in the saddle. Nineteen years later Nobody Told Me was ridden to victory by David Casey and the following year Mullins did it again, this time with Rule Supreme, with Casey once more in the saddle. Rule Supreme was an exceptionally versatile sort – he had won the Royal & SunAlliance Chase at Cheltenham three months earlier – and at Leopardstown the following February he took his trainer's extraordinary tally in the Hennessy Gold Cup to six in seven years.

Every jump jockey and trainer wants to win the Grand National, and Mullins had two mounts in the world's greatest steeplechase. Both were complete outsiders. He got as far as two fences before Becher's Brook on the second circuit on 200-1 shot The Lady's Master in 1983. The following season he teamed up with Hazy Dawn who, despite her win at Cheltenham, started at 100-1, but she got no further than Becher's first time round.

His first runner as a trainer was Micko's Dream, a horse owned by a syndicate of prison officers, and a first-fence faller in 2000. Alexander Banquet unseated his rider at Becher's two years later and in 2004 fell on the second circuit. That year Hedgehunter – owned by Trevor Hemmings, whose extensive business interests include Blackpool Tower – made much of the running, jumping like a stag for David Casey, and was still just about in contention when he fell at the final fence.

Mullins promptly set about preparing the horse for the 2005 race, shrewdly keeping him over hurdles until the Grand National weights had been published so that the handicapper did not get a chance to up the horse's mark over fences. Paddy Mullins, now retired, travelled with his wife to Aintree to see the race and savour the atmosphere. David Casey was injured this time and he had already been told that Ruby Walsh, as stable jockey, would replace him. Hedgehunter, a strong-looking bay gelding with a touch of finishing speed to complement his resolute stamina, started favourite. Those who backed him had an anxious moment when he made a mistake at the fence before Becher's on the second circuit and Walsh briefly lost a stirrup iron, but he jumped everything else every bit as well as he had done the previous year. Concentrating on settling the horse to preserve his energy, Walsh found himself in front much sooner than he wanted, at Becher's second time round, but he did not ask the favourite to go on and win his race until he reached the elbow on the run-in.

Hedgehunter proved to be a real Aintree specialist. In the 2006 Grand National, despite having to shoulder a huge weight, he beat all except Numbersixvalverde. The handicapper again showed him no mercy in 2007 – he had to give weight all round – but he completed the course to finish ninth.

With so many of his biggest wins coming outside Ireland, Willie Mullins has usually found the trainers' championship beyond him. In any case the title used to be decided by the number of races won rather than by the cumulative prize money. When the time came to change the system, it was left to the trainers themselves to decide the basis. Noel Meade, Mullins's principal rival for the title, said that it mattered little to him which method was used, but that Mullins must state his preference. According to Meade, Mullins hesitated and seemed unwilling to commit himself. In the event, while Mullins topped the prize money lists in 1999/2000 and again the following season, Meade has come out on top for both money and races won in subsequent campaigns.

For more than five years Mullins played an active role in racing politics as chairman of the Irish Racehorse Trainers' Association. 'Jim Bolger and John Oxx were chairman before me, and both are Flat trainers, whereas most of our members are country jumping trainers. I thought it was time one of these was made chairman and I felt I could give them more of a voice than a Flat trainer would.'

It was during Mullins's time as chairman that the Turf Club handed over many of its powers to state-sponsored bodies, first the Irish Horseracing Authority and then Horse Racing Ireland, in return for receiving the proceeds of off-course betting tax. This injection of cash was to transform racing's finances and give a huge financial boost to those working in the sport, but many in the Turf Club were reluctant to give up the authority which they and their predecessors had exercised for over 200 years.

In October 2000 Joe Walsh, Minister for Agriculture, announced that negotiations with the Turf Club had reached an impasse, and as a result he would find it difficult to recommend increased funding to the rest of the cabinet. This was too much for racing's Industry Group, of which Mullins was a leading participant, and it decided to stage a protest march on the day of the Turf Club's general meeting. Hundreds of stable staff, owners, trainers, breeders, jockeys and others who derived their living from racing converged on the Stand House Hotel at The Curragh from all over the country. They marched through the members' car park to the front of the grandstand where the general meeting was taking place in the St Leger suite. Several carried placards and they broke into chants of 'We want change' as Willie Mullins walked up the steps to deliver a letter of protest to chief executive Brian Kavanagh. When senior steward Gerry Scanlan refused to meet the protestors, he and his fellow stewards promptly came under attack from many of the Turf Club's own members. Two days later Scanlan and deputy senior steward Ray Rooney went to the Department of Agriculture headquarters in Dublin's Kildare Street to meet Walsh and Finance Minster Charlie McCreevy. They agreed to give up the Turf Club's registry office function in return for a minority representation on the state-sponsored body and an enormous increase in racing's funding.

After serving as chairman for two further years, Mullins decided to hand over the reins and concentrate solely on his training operation. He aims to continually upgrade the quality of his horses and, surprisingly perhaps, has spoken of an ambition to win a major Flat race. 'At one time I wanted a lot of Flat horses. Now I don't – jumpers are the main thing – and the money we are spending on Flat horses is bottom-of-the-barrel stuff, but my goal is to win a classic.'

Like many top trainers, Mullins has little interest in betting:

When I think a horse is a big price I might put my money where my mouth is, as I did with Florida Pearl in the King George VI Chase, but I hate losing. It doesn't bother me when my owners bet, provided they keep their winnings and losses to themselves. I find it hard, when a horse runs a tremendous race and finishes third, to hear the owner moaning about what he has lost in the ring. I prefer to talk about how well the horse ran.

This upbeat attitude is typical of Mullins's approach to life. He invariably begins his post-race press interviews by saying 'I was delighted with that.' He always accentuates the positive and tends to play up the prospects of his horses running well, if not actually winning. It's a school of thought that he has adopted over the years, rather than the result of any inbuilt optimism.

Racing is basically a game of disappointments. I believe that you have to grab the good things that happen and focus on these, otherwise you'll go off your head. Similarly I like to concentrate on the good things that might happen and to look forward. You have to take an upbeat view in this game and I like to look on the bright side all the time.

BIGGEST RACES WON

1995

Supreme Novices' Hurdle	Tourist Attraction

1996

Champion Bumper	Wither Or Which
Galway Hurdle	Mystical City

1997

Champion Bumper	Florida Pearl

1998

Royal & SunAlliance Chase	Florida Pearl
Champion Bumper	Alexander Banquet

1999

Leopardstown Hennessy Gold Cup	Florida Pearl

2000

Leopardstown Hennessy Gold Cup	Florida Pearl
Champion Bumper	Joe Cullen

2001

Leopardstown Hennessy Gold Cup	Florida Pearl
King George VI Chase	Florida Pearl

2002

Leopardstown Hennessy Gold Cup	Alexander Banquet
Triumph Hurdle	Scolardy
Punchestown Gold Cup	Florida Pearl

2003

Grande Course de Haies	Nobody Told Me

2004

Leopardstown Hennessy Gold Cup	Florida Pearl
Royal & SunAlliance Chase	Rule Supreme
Grande Course de Haies	Rule Supreme

2005

Leopardstown Hennessy Gold Cup	Rule Supreme
Champion Bumper	Missed That
Grand National	Hedgehunter

2007

Supreme Novices' Hurdle	Ebaziyan

4

JIM BOLGER

The Curragh, 28 June 1992. The Budweiser Irish Derby. St Jovite, in front shortly after halfway, draws further and further away in the straight to slam Epsom Derby winner Dr Devious by one of the biggest margins in the history of the race. The trainer of the runner-up remarks, 'The man who runs Irish racing has won.' The tongue-in-cheek comment might not have been an accurate one but it did refer to another facet of this remarkable trainer.

Jim Bolger has handled many famous horses but it is his attitude and approach towards the racing authorities that makes him stand apart from most others in his profession. A man with firm opinions and unshakeable convictions, he became convinced quite early in his career that it was wrong for racing to be run by a self-appointed, undemocratic body. Soon he was speaking out against the Turf Club and, to a lesser extent, the Racing Board. He took the former to court and won, his victory resulting in changes to the rules of racing. He has also made his mark as a tutor of both jockeys and trainers, with Tony McCoy and Aidan O'Brien the most famous names to have been schooled at his Coolcullen stables.

Born on Christmas Day 1941, Bolger was one of eight children of a farmer near Oylegate in County Wexford. He is related to authors Roddy Doyle and Maeve Brennan, and hard work was instilled into him as a way of life. He was expected to milk cows before setting off on a seven-mile cycle ride to school and, although he was quite young when he learned to ride, his father kept half-bred horses, not thoroughbreds. His passions as a boy were hurling (it still is and he will on occasion miss a Sunday race meeting to support Wexford at Croke Park) and Gaelic football. Those who knew him in those days recall a boy firmly convinced that he was right in whatever he did.

Bolger left school at seventeen to train as an accountant in Dublin, working in an office during the day and studying at the College of Commerce in Rathmines in the evening, but by this time he was hooked on racing and determined to become a trainer. He spent his holidays at the bloodstock sales in Ballsbridge, studying what legends like Vincent O'Brien and Paddy Prendergast looked for when they were buying yearlings. He got a job as an accountant with one of the main Ford dealers and in 1975, at the age of thirty-three with a wife and two small daughters to support, he started training under permit. A year later he packed in the job to take out a professional trainer's licence. Given his family commitments, it sounds a mammoth gamble, but Bolger did not see it that way. He had not the slightest doubt about his ability to make the grade in his chosen profession, nor did he consider the accountancy job all that secure. Apart from anything else, he found it difficult to settle into it when his mind was on racing and when he was spending almost as much time with his horses as he was in the office.

He operated from a rented yard in Clonsilla on the outskirts of Dublin and made rapid progress. In 1977 he won twenty-two races and at Aintree the following March put himself on the map by winning the Papermate Hurdle with Beparoejojo. He employed an attacking policy with his horses, going for whatever prizes he thought they could win. This, coupled with shrewd placing, brought a succession of good wins, even though his horses were useful rather than outstanding.

At the end of 1978 Sir Hugh Nugent retired from training and invited Bolger to take over his successful Lohunda Park stables, also in Clonsilla. In 1981 Bolger had his first really big wins on the Flat with a filly called Condessa, who won both the Musidora Stakes and the Yorkshire Oaks, and was also runner-up in the Irish Oaks. Even now, however, not everyone shared the trainer's belief in himself. Bolger recalls with wry amusement how he had overheard bloodstock agent Jack Doyle, who had bought Condessa before her Yorkshire Oaks win, saying his prayers as the filly was loaded into the stalls. 'Please God,' whispered Doyle. 'Don't let her be last.'

Bolger was rapidly outgrowing the stables at Lohunda Park and his mind was made up for him by a fire which ravaged much of the yard in 1982. He and wife Jackie began searching for new premises. The trainer wanted a place away from the main training centres, with hills where he could build the type of searching gallop that he now believed was necessary for training horses. They looked at forty-one farms before visiting Glebe House at Coolcullen, a tiny village on the Carlow/Kilkenny border. The farm had been built for the Bishop of Ossory in the eighteenth century, and Bolger bought it with 180 acres. In December 1982, with over a hundred boxes built and the gallops laid, the horses were moved from Clonsilla. They must have been surprised at the terrain over which they were expected to work. One section of the all-weather gallop is more than a mile long and rises 200 feet. Furthermore, unlike many of his rivals, Bolger built the gallop wide. He also made a mile-long grass gallop wider still so that it could be divided into sections for use at various times of the year. Three inches of peat was mixed into the surface of the outside strip to make it serviceable even at the height of summer.

Few trainers were able to match Bolger's horses for fitness, and within seven months he had his first classic winner, Give Thanks in the Irish Oaks, while Flame Of Tara won the Coronation Stakes at Royal Ascot. The following season Park Appeal won both the Moyglare Stud Stakes and the Cheveley Park, in 1986 Park Express won the Phoenix Champion Stakes, and the following season Polonia proved herself to be one of the best sprinters in Europe by landing the Prix de l'Abbaye at Longchamp.

In 1990 Bolger broke Senator Jim Parkinson's 1923 record of 134 winners in a calendar year and the following season Jet Ski Lady sprang a 50-1 shock in the Oaks. However, the best was still to come. St Jovite, a long-striding bay with hardly any white on him, looked decidedly sluggish in his first two races of 1992 and it was no surprise to see him beaten two lengths by Dr Devious in the Derby. What was a surprise was that he reversed the form at The Curragh in such sensational style. Bolger ran two others in the Irish Derby to ensure a strong pace and Christy Roche sent St Jovite to the front fully five furlongs from home. John Reid on Dr Devious tried to get to him in the straight but the Bolger horse simply found another gear, increasing his advantage all the way to the line to slam his Epsom conqueror by twelve lengths in record time.

It was a staggering performance. Only once before had a horse won Ireland's richest race by such a wide margin – Portmarnock, back in 1895 – while the time of 2 minutes 25.6 seconds was three seconds faster than the previous course record. Three seconds is the equivalent of fifty yards, and the record was widely disbelieved. Timing experts in the media had hand-timed the race at around 2 minutes 26 seconds and, since this showed that there was not much wrong with the clock, they were convinced that the distance must have been less than the official mile and a half. This view was given credence when the clerk of the course admitted that the track had not been measured since the previous year's race. However, racecourse manager Jim Marsh walked the course with a measuring wheel the following day and was relieved to find that the race had been run over the full twelve furlongs.

Further controversy had arisen when Christy Roche was allowed to take the ride on St Jovite. Bolger's stable jockey had been suspended for fifteen days, and two days before the race he went to the High Court in a bid to obtain an injunction preventing his appeal being heard until after the Irish Derby. The injunction was refused, but the stewards then made what they called 'an enlightened gesture' to postpone the hearing and allow Roche to ride in the race. The stewards were widely criticised for climbing down, but Roche was a relieved man. He knew that St Jovite had improved out of all recognition since Epsom, and he was worried that American jockey Cash Asmussen would take his place.

Cash was one of the jockeys on the phone for the ride, and I feared that if I was suspended it would have meant the beginning of the end so far as my career was concerned. People would have compared me pushing from a long way out at Epsom to the colt's runaway win at The Curragh. They would have said that no horse could improve that much – it must be the jockey. Cash would almost certainly have kept the ride in St Jovite's future races, and I had sleepless nights worrying about the situation.

When the appeal was finally heard, the Turf Club stewards showed Roche no mercy, upholding the original ban and ordering him to pay £5,000 costs. Roche went back to the High Court and this time he was successful in obtaining an injunction. This allowed him to ride in the Irish Oaks, but on the eve of the King George VI and Queen Elizabeth Diamond Stakes, Justice Declan Costello, the acting president of the High Court, said that he was not prepared to grant a further injunction and that the remaining twelve days of the suspension were to begin immediately. Stephen Craine took over on St Jovite in the big Ascot race and the colt won easily.

The unfortunate horse seemed to be dogged by rows and controversy. He was owned and bred by Virginia Kraft Payson, a formidable American woman who proved to be every bit as strong-willed as her trainer. When it came to the Breeders' Cup Classic at Gulfstream Park in Florida in October 1992, she insisted that Roche be replaced by American jockey Laffit Pincay. It was not an unreasonable decision.

American races are run on courses of which European riders have little experience, and this has often proved to be a decisive factor at Breeders' Cup meetings.

Bolger is fiercely loyal to his stable jockeys and hates any attempt by owners to replace them with riders of their own choosing, but on this occasion he was prepared to give way to Mrs Kraft Payson. However, St Jovite picked up a respiratory infection and was unable to travel to Florida. This did not go down well with the owner, who demanded an independent veterinary examination. Although apparently satisfied by the results, she insisted that the horse be sent to America for a break. Bolger and his wife went out there the following February, and submitted a campaign programme for the horse which they believed to be accepted by the owner. But St Jovite broke down in a racecourse workout and was rushed off to stud. Virginia Kraft Payson then removed the other two horses she had with Bolger and she never sent him another.

It was obvious that the relationship between owner and trainer had broken down irretrievably; Bolger believes, however, that Mrs Kraft Payson may have heard 'the rumours about my impending bankruptcy'. He was referring to the ill-starred flotation of GPA, a giant aircraft leasing company, in which several wealthy men lost fortunes. Bolger was widely believed to have been one of them. 'There was no truth in that whatsoever. The knockers had me investing everything I had in GPA but I never had tuppence invested,' he says. 'The financial controller's name was Bolger but the rumours were more to do with Maurice Foley, the president, being my brother-in-law.'

When Park Appeal won the 1984 Moyglare Stud Stakes at The Curragh, Bolger gained the right to make a speech at the Moyglare Dinner three months later. He took full advantage, in an outspoken manner never before matched by any trainer at a public function. He scathingly attacked the Turf Club and its programmes committee, and then hammered the Racing Board, the state-sponsored body which had responsibility for much of racing's finances. 'It is not fighting a losing battle, it has thrown in the towel,' Bolger told his audience.

The speech went down like a lead balloon with many members of the racing establishment. When Bolger's yard was shut down by a virus early the following season, they regarded it as a supremely appropriate form of divine retribution, as well as a stark reminder to the upstart from County Carlow that God was a paid-up member of the Establishment.

Bolger had no regrets. Nor did his view of the authorities mellow; if anything, the opposite. In an address to the Eastern Region of the Irish Thoroughbred Breeders' Association in Kilkenny in January 1990, he launched an even more blistering attack:

Racing in Ireland today is governed by the Turf Club and Irish National Hunt Steeplechase Committee, a club where pedigree counts for more than performance, where no politician is welcome, where fourteen per cent are ex one army or the other, where fifteen per cent have a close relation to keep things cosy and where only two per cent are female. It will surprise many to know that a large body of Turf Club members are neither owners of racehorses now or in the recent past in Ireland, and that some have chosen to have their horses trained in England. Can you imagine how pathetic a plea for help from such a body to our government must sound in Kildare Street [the Dublin offices of the Department of Agriculture]? You cannot join our club but you must help us.

Bolger admits that he anticipated reprisals – 'the speech was at a weekend and I expected to be called to the Turf Club by the following Friday' – but there were none. Almost a decade earlier he had sat on the same table as members of the Turf Club, as a member of the Killanin Commission of Inquiry into the Thoroughbred Horse

Breeding Industry. Chaired by Olympic Games supremo Lord Killanin, this was a painstaking and far-reaching examination which finally saw the light of day in 1986. It was an influential document that was widely regarded as a blueprint for the future. The meeting with Turf Club members took place in Dublin's Shelbourne Hotel:

> They arrived late and I asked them whether the Turf Club did not think that women had anything to contribute to Irish racing, and did they not think that the Turf Club should be representative of Irish racegoers in general, of whom quite a lot are women. They looked at each other and nobody bothered to answer the question. However, some months later Sonia Rogers became the first female member of the Turf Club.

Equally, Bolger admits to having felt critical of the Turf Club long before he made his Moyglare dinner speech in 1984:

> It was as soon as I had my eyes opened and saw what was going on, but never at any stage was there anything personal against any of the members. In addition, I have always had a good relationship with the staff. It was the set-up I was against.
>
> I never felt that I would have such an influence on the Turf Club. I asked about their accounts and eventually these were published. Some time after I spoke in Kilkenny about the cosy cartel they began to elect the senior steward. I suppose I prolonged their existence by pointing out the changes that needed to be made. Having made those changes, the Turf Club is now more acceptable than it was, and I am happy to see that their role has been reduced to that of the whistle on racedays.

In August 1990 Bolger fell foul of the stewards in Dundalk. His Nordic Tiara, ridden by Christy Roche, won a modest two-year-old maiden race. Second was Ashco, ridden by Seamus Heffernan, and the racecourse stewards ruled that this little-fancied stable companion had not been run on her merits, suggesting by implication that Ashco could have won had she been ridden to do so. Under Rule 148 (i), which stated that 'a trainer shall be responsible for everything connected with the running of a horse trained by him', Bolger was fined £500 and Heffernan suspended for five days. There was an appeal against the sentence, and although Bolger went to the High Court and secured an injunction preventing the Turf Club stewards from hearing that appeal, the court later decided that they were entitled to hold it. The stewards confirmed Heffernan's suspension, ruling that he had made insufficient effort, but they also found that Bolger was not responsible for Ashco not being ridden on her merits. It was an important victory, but the Turf Club decided to make no change to Rule 148. Bolger considered the rule to be unjust and was determined to fight. 'Even God only holds you responsible for your own actions.'

Racing's rule book is bigger and more complex than those of other sports. Transgressions for minor offences are commonplace and those convicted often appeal, with varying degrees of success. Bolger repeatedly refused to do so, maintaining that 'I have no faith in the appeals system.' However, he made an exception after an incident at Naas in July 1994, deciding if necessary to pursue his case through the courts. The race was another two-year-old maiden and, as at Dundalk, Seamus Heffernan was on the second string. Bolger's son-in-law Kevin Manning rode Pozzoli, who started hot favourite and won the race; Heffernan was on Tirolean, a newcomer who started at 12-1 and was only beaten a head. Many at the County Kildare course that evening thought that Heffernan's mount might well have won had he been given a more forceful ride (the Turf Club form book commented that Tirolean was 'hand-ridden'). The colt made the early running and ran on strongly at the end, despite not even being shown the whip.

Asked by the press if he did not think that Tirolean would have won had more pressure been applied, Bolger was adamant that he was satisfied with Heffernan's riding. 'This was Tirolean's first run,' he said. 'It's conjecture as to whether he would have won [if he had been ridden more vigorously]. None of us can know that. Don't forget all the hassle there was over the last one [Ashco]. She never won again.'

The racecourse stewards held a lengthy inquiry – by this time Bolger had a reputation as a formidable adversary, and the stewards knew they could be in trouble if they failed to go through all the proper procedures – and they suspended Heffernan for twenty-eight days, gave Tirolean a thirty-day ban and fined Bolger £1,000. At the subsequent appeal hearing, which lasted for six hours, the Turf Club stewards did not accept Heffernan's explanation – that he was not harder on Tirolean because he could hear the horse gurgling – to be an adequate excuse. They ruled that the original sentences should stand because they were satisfied that Tirolean had not complied with Rule 212. This states that every horse must be run on its merits; since it ensures fair play, it is the most important rule in the book. However, the stewards also relied on Rule 148 (i), which the trainer was determined to fight.

I had right on my side and whenever you have that you are a long way down the road to success. I hadn't expected a positive result at the Turf Club's appeal hearing and I had made up my mind beforehand that it would be a good idea to go further because I felt I should have been exonerated at Naas. I didn't do anything wrong and I believed that what Seamus Heffernan told me about the horse gurgling was the truth.

I wanted to pick a good one [case to appeal] and this was it. I had everything right, including a witness in the parade ring when I gave the riding instructions. The instructions were not carried out, but I accepted the jockey's explanation as to why they were not. Taking into account what Seamus told me, I was satisfied with the ride. I also had a very good legal team in my solicitor Nuala MacKenzie and senior counsel Kevin Haugh.

Kevin set the scene at the Turf Club. He brought the noose with him and they [the appeal stewards] willingly put their heads into it: they were warned at the outset that, if they found against me, they would have to give reasons and they stubbornly refused to do so. The way the hearing was carried out was an absolute disgrace.

At the end of the hearing, Kevin Haugh asked that the findings should include a statement that no misconduct had been found against Bolger. This the stewards refused to do, and in what Bolger described as 'an expensive gamble', he decided to go to the High Court. This would be hugely expensive if he failed to win the case: the Turf Club's costs were eventually estimated at over £100,000 and his own would not be much less. Bolger had become a wealthy man by this stage but, even so, a bill for over £200,000 would have hit him hard. 'I did give consideration to the costs but I felt they were never going to be my baby,' he says with extraordinary self-belief. 'But I couldn't believe that the Turf Club went ahead with the case, although I was hoping they would because I had no intention of settling it. That would have meant that we were back to the status quo with a stupid rule.'

The Turf Club stewards had little alternative other than to fight it out in court. To climb down, particularly against their bitterest opponent, would have been supreme cowardice. In any case the members of the panel who sat in judgement at the appeal – Michael Osborne, Frank Hardy, Michael Dargan and Seamus McGrath – were men of principle and high integrity. They had the rules of racing to uphold; they believed in those rules and in their case. Bolger brought his action against these four men as well as against the Turf Club. Sadly, all four of the quartet are now dead.

There is a huge backlog of cases in the High Court and this one took nearly five years to complete. Part of the reason was that Kevin Haugh was appointed a district judge, and his replacement, after working on the case for several months, found that he was not going to be available. Nuala MacKenzie then picked Eoghan Fitzsimons, a former Attorney General. With so much at stake for Bolger, he might have been expected to take every opportunity to impress on Fitzsimons the machinations of the rule book and how they should be interpreted, if not actually to play a leading part in deciding how the case should be presented. He refrained from doing so. 'That would have been like giving riding instructions to Lester Piggott. We talked through the case beforehand and I told Eoghan everything I felt he needed to know but, as regards the format of how he was going to run with it, that was all his work.'

Bolger did not take the witness stand, nor did he appear in court when Justice Fidelma Macken gave her verdict on 6 August 1999. 'I chose not to give evidence because we had it in the bag by that stage, and I was only interested in clearing my name and showing up the rule, not in any damages.'

The judge ruled comprehensively against the Turf Club. Furthermore, she said, Bolger was entitled to some sort of reason for the appeal decision – 'the transcript of the hearing makes it clear that no evidence was given that he was at fault'. She also indicated that she was unhappy with Rule 148 (i), particularly when read in conjunction with the 'non-triers' rule of 212, adding that 'there is a starting point at which the trainer is liable. He then has to prove that he was not responsible. Any ambiguity should be interpreted in favour of the plaintiff [Bolger]. It seems to me that a finding of liability against the plaintiff was wholly irrational and unsustainable.'

Justice Macken decided against awarding any damages to Bolger, pointing out that he had given no evidence of having suffered damage – 'I do not, therefore, think I should make any award for general damages to his good name which has now been vindicated.'

The Turf Club considered an appeal to the Supreme Court, but it took little more than a fortnight for the stewards and their lawyers to decide to accept the verdict. They then set about changing Rule 148 (i), adding to the section asserting the trainer's liability for everything connected with the running of a horse trained by him or her the words 'and shall be liable to any sanction available to the stewards unless the trainer provides a satisfactory explanation'. It was a sensible solution, but those who hoped for any sort of magnanimity from the victor were to be disappointed. Bolger, interviewed immediately after the Turf Club's announcement that it would not go to the Supreme Court and would change the rule, was more critical than ever:

> This was a serious setback for the Turf Club. Not only is it a self-perpetuating club but it is also an inept one. They wheeled out the best they could on the day [of the appeal] and this was the best effort they could do in dispensing justice, something they are supposed to do in a fair and impartial way. They patently failed to do that. The findings of Justice Fidelma Macken, that the hearing at the Turf Club was 'wholly irrational and unsustainable', are damning words for a body that has been running the regulatory side of racing for 200 years.

Every racing stable of any size attracts teenage hopefuls anxious to make a career as a jockey or a trainer. Many trainers give the youngsters little opportunity to progress beyond a stable staff job, but Jim Bolger is one of the exceptions. It has always been his practice to reward talent and hard work with race-riding opportunities, and this policy has put many jockeys on the road to success. These include Tony McCoy, Willie Supple, Ted Durcan, Dean Gallagher, Seamus Heffernan and Kevin Manning. Paul Carberry also spent part of his apprenticeship at Coolcullen, and Aidan O'Brien played an increasingly important role during his time there. They all speak of Bolger as firm but fair. He made them start at 7 a.m., worked them hard, warned them that smoking and drinking were banned, and encouraged them to go to mass several times a week. He takes pride in the way the best of them have turned out.

I am very anxious for them to achieve in life and I set out with them in much the same way that I do with the horses. If a person is capable of 100, taking a scale of nought to 100, I am keen that he achieves that, as Aidan O'Brien did. If you have somebody with a lesser IQ and not the same capacity for work or endurance, I am happy if they achieve 50 if that is their maximum. What I hate to see is somebody with talent dropping out and going into other lines of business, and I've had a few of these. It gives me no satisfaction to have had people who haven't achieved their full potential.

A jockey can show you as an apprentice what he might be capable of but it is difficult to predict who will make a trainer. Some trainers get fond of the good life once they have had a bit of success and then don't work as hard. Others just don't have the talent. Aidan and Tony McCoy were both top drawer when they were with me, although I didn't expect either of them to go on and achieve what they have.

It is not only his staff who are banned from smoking and drinking. Any pressman going into the winner's enclosure with a cigarette in his hand can expect a rude reception. Bolger's hatred of both drink and tobacco stems not so much from a puritanical streak as from what he has seen them do to other people. He used to visit an elderly former trainer in a hospice, and was shocked to find that cancer caused by smoking had made the poor man incontinent. He was also well aware of the battle Nicky Rackard, the great Wexford hurler, had to fight to overcome alcohol addiction.

The late Raymond Smith, in his book *Tigers of the Turf*, wrote that, after interviewing Bolger, 'I was left with a distinct feeling that he would benefit from taking a glass or two of vintage claret, and that it would make him relax more.' Bolger does not agree that he would be more relaxed if he had a drink in the evenings. 'I have a great capacity to unwind and I have other interests outside racing. I believe it is very important for anyone in a sport as demanding as ours to have outside interests. For my part, I am interested in what goes on in the world.'

Bolger is an exceptionally hard worker and is up at 6.15 a.m. each day. He has continued riding work at an age when even trainers who used to be jockeys have stopped doing so. His one concession to advancing age is to go racing less often, although he attributes this to the dangers posed by the constantly increasing traffic levels on Irish roads.

Alexander Goldrun won Group One races in 2004 and again in the following two years, thus ending a period when the Bolger horses seemed to have trouble competing at the top level. Many of his string are bred either by himself or in conjunction with Harry Dobson, and the majority do not have the pedigrees to compete with the bluebloods of Ballydoyle.

> Looking at it realistically, I would have a couple of million pounds' worth of yearlings each year and the Coolmore/Ballydoyle outfit would have almost £100 million worth. I therefore need a large injection of luck to get one that is going to upset their horses. But I'm glad I got a run when Vincent O'Brien hung up his binoculars. When I started out, I never dreamed that one day I would be champion trainer.

The Scottish-born Dobson made his fortune from zinc mines in Canada. He had a sizeable stake in Manchester United when John Magnier's dispute with Sir Alex Ferguson was its height, and sold out at much the same time as the Magnier/J.P. McManus alliance. He also knows Bolger better than anyone outside his immediate family, and his views, even though they were expressed to the author back in 2001, are informative:

> We go back a long way but for the last ten years we have muddled away with pedigrees that are so far behind everyone else's that it's not funny. However, we have had a lot of success and this is because of his training. There is no question in my mind that he is the best in Ireland,

and I include Aidan O'Brien in that. He doesn't have the tools that Aidan, Dermot Weld and John Oxx have, but he competes with them. If he takes them on, he feels he can beat them. He doesn't always do so but he believes he can.

All this stuff with the Turf Club was totally well meant and for quite some time his was a lonely voice battling against everything. He got support in a quiet way but very few people were prepared to put their heads above the parapet like he did, and he deserves a lot of credit for that.

Also he is the only man I have ever known who has never had one moment of self-doubt, at least on the surface. We all think from time to time that maybe we got something wrong, but if Jim were to admit to getting it wrong, you would know that he is joking. Probably his weakness is that he is always absolutely certain that he is correct.

It is a fascinating assessment, and in 2006 Bolger proved beyond doubt that he still has what it takes to compete at the top level when he came up with two exceptional two-year-olds in Finsceal Beo and Teofilo. The latter was ante-post favourite for the following season's 2,000 Guineas and Derby, but a setback ruled him out of both races. However, Finsceal Beo did her trainer proud. She won the 1,000 Guineas, came within inches of adding the French equivalent and then landed the Irish version – all in three weeks.

BIGGEST RACES WON

1981

Yorkshire Oaks	Condessa

1983

Coronation Stakes	Flame Of Tara

Irish Oaks   Give Thanks

1984
Moyglare Stud Stakes   Park Appeal
Cheveley Park Stakes   Park Appeal

1986
Phoenix Champion Stakes   Park Express

1987
Prix de l'Abbaye   Polonia

1991
Oaks   Jet Ski Lady

1992
Irish Derby   St Jovite
King George VI and Queen Elizabeth Stakes St Jovite

1994
Phoenix Stakes   Eva Luna

1995
Moyglare Stud Stakes   Priory Belle

1996
Phoenix Stakes   Mantovani

2002
Irish Oaks   Margarula

2004
Prix de l'Opera   Alexander Goldrun

Hong Kong Cup   Alexander Goldrun

2005
Pretty Polly Stakes   Alexander Goldrun
Nassau Stakes   Alexander Goldrun

2006
Pretty Polly Stakes   Alexander Goldrun
National Stakes   Teofilo
Prix Marcel Boussac   Finsceal Beo
Dewhurst Stakes   Teofilo

2007
1,000 Guineas   Finsceal Beo
Irish 1,000 Guineas   Finsceal Beo

5

DESSIE HUGHES

Cheltenham, 16 March 2004. Hardy Eustace, an unconsidered 33-1 chance, leads the Champion Hurdle field from the start. Amazingly, he is still just in front as the field sweeps towards the final flight, but the favourite is bearing down on him and draws level as the pair reach the hurdle. All those who have backed Rooster Booster start to cheer him home, but to their horror the blinkered Hardy Eustace finds another gear and powers home up the stamina-sapping final hill for a shock five-length victory.

Dessie Hughes, trainer of Hardy Eustace, is one of only three men to have both ridden and trained winners of the Champion Hurdle. He was a top-flight National Hunt jockey, but he took a long time to become a well-known name and for the best part of a decade it looked as if he was not going to make the grade. His training career, in contrast, got off to a flying start before a virus took a vice-like grip on the health of his horses and threatened to force him out of the game. It took him nearly ten years to find a cure and prove to owners that he still had what it takes to win races of the highest class.

Born on 10 October 1943, Desmond Hughes was only fourteen when he left school to go into racing. He was brought up in the Dublin suburb of Whitehall, where as a boy he saw few horses, and he had no family connection with the sport to help him achieve his ambition of becoming a jockey. His brother, Vincent, was equally keen on racing but his career was to centre on the administrative aspect of the sport; he has spent most of his working life in the offices of the Turf Club.

Young Dessie was apprenticed to Dan Kirwan in County Kilkenny. Kirwan won the 1933 Irish Grand National on Red Park, and he was the son of John Kirwan, who trained Heirdom to win the same race twelve years later. Such a solid National Hunt background made Kirwan's yard look an ideal place for a budding jump jockey, but Hughes was still without a winner when his boss died in 1960. He transferred his indentures to Willie O'Grady, and he was still full of optimism. After all, he was only seventeen. He rode a winner on the Flat and another over fences, but eventually he realised that he was going nowhere struggling for rides in Ireland where there was so little racing and the competition for mounts was so intense. He spotted an advertisement placed by Eugene Ferris, who trained at Lockerbie, the Dumfriesshire town that in December 1988 was to witness one of Britain's worst air disasters, in which 270 people lost their lives.

Ferris's was a little-known stable but it hit form soon after Hughes joined it, and he rode four winners inside two months. The latest Irish jump jockey to arrive on the British scene caught the attention of both the media and other trainers. Among those impressed was Reg Akehurst, himself a former jump jockey, who trained both on the Flat and over jumps at Baydon in Wiltshire. He offered Hughes a job as stable jockey for his National Hunt horses, and the twenty-two-year-old Irishman had good reason for assuming he had the world at his feet when he moved south at the beginning of 1966. However, he ended that year lying on his back in St Margaret's Hospital in Swindon. As a result of a terrible fall at Wolverhampton, both his lungs were punctured and he suffered serious damage to his back. It was almost three months before he was able to leave hospital, and that brief blaze of glory on Ferris's horses had already been forgotten by everyone except himself and the Scottish trainer. The Akehurst job, which had promised so much, produced precious few winners and

Hughes's total was still in single figures. 'By this stage I didn't think I was going to make it as a jump jockey, but I wanted it so much that I was determined not to give up trying. I had never had anything in my head other than wanting to be a jockey.'

He returned to Ireland, where a chance meeting with Mick O'Toole resulted in both a job and a resurgence of the earlier optimism. O'Toole, having begun his training career with greyhounds, had only recently made the switch to horses when Hughes went to work in his stables adjoining Dublin's Phoenix Park. Widely and accurately described as an irrepressible optimist, O'Toole is an entertaining character who worked hard to propel himself up the racing ladder. He moved to The Curragh once he began sending out winners, and he built up a powerful yard at Maddenstown. He won races at Royal Ascot and a classic with Dickens Hill, but it was success at Cheltenham for which he was best known.

All this was in the future when Hughes joined him, but the rapidly increasing number of horses meant there were opportunities on the racecourse. However, there was no second burst of winners for the young jockey such as he had achieved with Ferris. Indeed he went for nearly two and a half years without another success. 'Opportunities weren't as easy in those days,' he recalls in his distinctive deep and slightly throaty tones. 'There were more jockeys and a lot less racing than there is today, and you didn't get rides unless they were on horses that nobody else wanted to ride. I was twenty-seven or twenty-eight before I started to get recognised.' However, by 1970 he had progressed to the extent that he had a mount in the Grand National.

I rode Persian Helen for Mick. Every jump jockey wants to ride in the National, it's a great experience, and the fences are totally different from those in other races. Horses have to take tremendous leaps to get over them, and every fence brings a grunt from your mount. Also you are not in control. In most races you can aim to get into the position you want, but in the National you are just carried along once the flag goes up. With forty runners, they go off as fast as they can because everyone is trying to get a position, and usually you find yourself where you don't want to be.

Persian Helen was a 33-1 chance, and I found it a nerve-racking occasion. I was anticipating what was going to happen. I knew I was going to jump a few and then fall, and I was wondering which fence I was going to go at – obviously it's different when you are riding a good horse who is a sound leaper. Once we jumped off, the nervousness went, but there was a melee at the third fence. It's got a ditch in front of it and it's a very big fence, too big for a lot of horses. Mine got over it, but at the next two loose horses ran across me. She couldn't jump the fence, and she refused.

In 1974 Hughes won some decent races on Flashy Boy, a good two-mile chaser trained in County Armagh by Archie Watson, and the following March he had his first Cheltenham winner on Davy Lad in the SunAlliance Novices' Hurdle. Interestingly, and despite all his subsequent triumphs, he regards this as his greatest moment as a jockey. 'It was better than winning the Gold Cup or the Champion Hurdle, and my second best moment was my first winner, Sailaway Sailor, in a Flat race at Ballinrobe.'

Less than five months after that first Cheltenham success Hughes landed the Galway Plate, on Our Albert. By this time he was riding most of O'Toole's jumpers, and at the 1976 Cheltenham Festival the pair won both the SunAlliance Novices' Hurdle (with Parkhill) and the Lloyds Bank (later renamed the Stayers') Hurdle with Bit Of A Jig. The 1977 meeting was even better for Hughes, who rode three winners, including the Cheltenham Gold Cup on Davy Lad.

O'Toole, a fearless punter, had put £500 on the horse at 50-1 nearly three months beforehand. Davy Lad started at 14-1 and was probably lucky to win. The strongly fancied Lanzarote broke his hind leg and brought down the favourite, Bannow Rambler, while Summerville, going better than anything three fences from home, broke down at the next fence.

O'Toole had an even bigger bet on Davy Lad in the Grand National, but no horse had completed the Gold Cup–Grand National double in the same season since Golden Miller forty-three years earlier, and the money did not last long.

Davy Lad was the only decent horse I rode in the National, and there was a long delay at the start because of a protest [a demonstration on behalf of a local prisoner]. The race came only sixteen days after the Gold Cup and Davy Lad, always a lazy horse, was off the bridle after jumping only two fences. He'd had enough by the time he got to the third fence. He half refused, caught the top of it and fell.

War Bonnet the following year was my only other ride in the National. He was a 50-1 chance and he also fell at the third. You got a special fee for riding in the race, and I can remember some jockeys asking for plenty, £600 or even £1,000. Some of them got it, and some of them didn't. I think I was paid £300, but you would accept £100 if you were going bad and were glad of a ride.

In the race before the 1977 Grand National, won by Red Rum for the third time with Tommy Stack in the saddle, Hughes rode Monksfield in a thriller for the Templegate Hurdle. This gallant horse had been beaten two lengths by Night Nurse in the Champion Hurdle and was the ride of Mick Kinane's father, Tommy. However, Kinane was injured, and with Hughes very much in form he was an obvious choice for the ride. And he succeeded in forcing a dead-heat with Night Nurse.

The following season Kinane and Monksfield won the Champion Hurdle, beating Sea Pigeon, but twelve days later Kinane crushed several vertebrae in a fall in the Irish National. Hughes seized his chance with both hands at Aintree, and although Night Nurse started favourite for the Templegate, Monksfield beat him by two lengths.

Monksfield's connections used the Erin Foods Champion Hurdle at Leopardstown as their prep race for the 1979 Champion Hurdle, but the horse trailed in a disappointing sixth, prompting immediate recriminations. Trainer Des McDonogh instructed Kinane to hold the horse up longer than usual, but the race was run at a slow pace and the instructions meant that Monksfield's stamina could not be brought to bear. McDonogh thought that Kinane should have used his initiative instead of sticking to what he had been told, while the jockey was convinced the instructions were part of a conspiracy to get rid of him. The upshot was that Hughes replaced Kinane at Cheltenham, where he was to join one of the select band of jockeys to have won both the Gold Cup and the Champion Hurdle. The pair again followed up at Aintree. There was expected to be another epic battle with Sea Pigeon in the 1980 Champion Hurdle, but Monksfield's powers were beginning to wane and he was left for dead when his old rival swept past early on the run-in.

One of the lasting impressions of Hughes's handling of Monksfield was the rider's style and determination. The photographs confirm this. Despite being 5ft 10in, tall even for a jump jockey, Hughes rode finish after finish on this horse as if defeat was a word that did not exist. Little wonder that writer Raymond Smith eloquently described him as 'lean, like a gunfighter, and as deadly'.

Hughes's only winner at the 1980 Cheltenham Festival came on Chinrullah, who romped home twenty-five lengths clear in the Queen Mother Champion Chase. Sadly, the horse was disqualified two months later after traces of caffeine and theobromine showed up in his urine sample, the result of a batch of contaminated feedstuffs that also claimed Tied Cottage's Cheltenham Gold Cup victory.

Hughes had started training the previous year at a small yard he bought at Brownstown, on the same side of The Curragh as O'Toole's Maddenstown stables. He had a far more thorough grounding for his new career than most jockeys; having continued working with the O'Toole horses when he was promoted to stable jockey, he had spent many non-racing days tending to the legs of those who were temporarily sidelined. He had his first winner as a trainer with Church Island at Fairyhouse on New Year's Day 1980. He rode the horse himself, but he found riding and training a strain: 'When I was riding my own horses it felt as if I had 12st 7lb to carry every time.'

Just as big a concern was the yard at Brownstown. It was too small for Hughes's fast-growing string, and it did not have enough land. He then heard that Dermot Hurley wanted to sell Osborne Lodge and its surrounding acreage. Osborne Lodge, on the other side of The Curragh from Brownstown and beyond the racecourse, had been built at the end of the nineteenth century. Several classic winners were trained there, and it was just the sort of yard that Hughes hoped to have one day. Buying it so early in his training career was way beyond him financially, but O'Toole encouraged him to put in a bid, and he offered to buy the Brownstown yard to help him raise the money. (Later, when his own numbers declined, O'Toole sold his Maddenstown stables to the Irish National Stud and moved his horses into the Brownstown yard.) It did not take long for Hughes to fill the Osborne Lodge boxes and by the beginning of 1981 he had nearly fifty horses, the vast majority of them jumpers.

The large turnover that the training fees generated was vital to meeting the repayments on the money he had borrowed to buy his new yard, and a succession of good winners meant that there was plenty of demand for his services. He won the 1981 Irish Lincolnshire with Dellersbeck, and the gelding followed up in the Downshire Hurdle at the Punchestown Festival. Light The Wad also played a big part that year, winning the Arkle Chase at Leopardstown and the Motor Import Handicap Chase at Punchestown.

The following March Hughes trained his first Cheltenham winner when Miller Hill got the Irish off to a flier by springing a 20-1 surprise in the Supreme Novices' Hurdle. 'I had a fabulous start as a trainer. I had a lot of very good horses and, luckily enough, a jockey in Tom Morgan who was brilliant. I had a great time for five or six years.'

Chow Mein won the 1985 Galway Plate, and the following year Hughes had thirty-one winners under National Hunt rules alone. Only Paddy Mullins and Pat Hughes trained more winners, and the Osborne Lodge prize money total took its owner into seventh place in the lists. Some quieter years followed, even though Charlie Swan joined the stable, but Hughes was comfortably back into the top ten both in 1991/92 and in the following season, before it all started to go pear-shaped. He had just seven winners in the 1993/94 campaign, twelve in the following season and eleven in 1995/96. It was a grim time for Hughes and his wife Eileen. One of the few compensations was the success of their son, Richard, who was doing well as a Flat race jockey despite being as tall as his father – Willie Carson nicknamed him the window cleaner – and having to subject himself to intense deprivation to ride at 8st 6lb. The Hugheses' daughter, Sandra, married another Flat race rider, John Egan, and the way his son and son-in-law were clocking up the winners brought home to Dessie Hughes the difference between life as a jockey and as a trainer.

> Training is fantastic when you have a good horse, and he wins. The rest of it is very hard work, with problems and headaches. A jockey's life is fantastic if you like doing it, and I loved it. Every day I wished that I was still a jockey. When you don't have many winners, people go to other trainers with their horses. You develop a guilt complex when you know your horses are not right, and you can't get them right.

Hughes knew he had a virus in the yard but neither he nor his vets could put their fingers on a cure. He tried resting his horses, and they seemed to come back healthy. Some of them won races, though more of them failed to produce as much as he thought them capable of. He was not the only one with this problem, of course. No trainer ever escapes what is known as 'the virus', but it comes in many different forms. Often it is not much worse than the common cold, and may or may not be accompanied by a cough. On other occasions it's more like flu, with the horses running a temperature. Horses asked to race when they are incubating the virus will run way below their best, and they can do irreparable damage to their breathing systems in the process. However, the real problem comes when they give every sign of being fit and healthy but cannot perform to their best, and this is what affected those at Osborne Lodge.

Hughes heard the stories about Vincent O'Brien having similar problems in his last few years as a trainer, and about how the virus seemed to take a grip in the actual walls of other trainers' stables. Just as they had done, he power-hosed the boxes with disinfectant. When this did not work, he tried different brands. He then moved his horses from Osborne Lodge to Mountjoy Lodge, another yard on the same side of The Curragh, once owned by legendary jockey Steve Donoghue and more recently by Stephen Quirke and Tony Redmond. The horses quickly picked up, but they went steadily downhill again after returning to Osborne Lodge. More and more owners lost faith in Hughes, and his numbers dwindled as they moved their horses to other yards. At one point he was down to sixteen horses, and close to despair.

> Training horses is not that difficult if they are healthy, if you are careful and if you give them plenty of thought. But not even the best trainer in the world will train plenty of winners when he has a viral infection in the yard, and I had come to realise that the virus is the worst aspect of being a trainer. I came very close to believing that I would have to give up. I put a lot of thought into moving down the country somewhere but buying the land, building stables and a house would have been very expensive. And I wondered who would buy Osborne Lodge. The only person would be another trainer but nobody would want a yard with a virus, and we had a history of it.

It was the Irish Equine Centre that finally got to the root of the problem and came up with a solution that worked. The Centre, based at Johnston in County Kildare, is a diagnostic and research laboratory whose purpose is to serve the needs of the country's bloodstock and racing industries. Tom Buckley, the Centre's head of microbiology, diagnosed a fungus infection called aspergilus that affects buildings, particularly old ones, and is normally associated with chicken houses. Hughes believes that it got into Osborne Lodge as a result of straw that was either bad or damp.

Buckley was able to come up with an antidote, which was used when the boxes were power-hosed. This was done every three weeks and swabs taken after the cleaning process came up negative throughout 2000, whereas they had previously tested positive. The number of winners produced by the stable steadily increased, reaching thirty in the 2001/02 season for the first time in a decade. 'I would sometimes look back and think what we might have won if we hadn't had that virus. I know that we had a lot of very good horses that I couldn't properly train, and it was dreadful for them.'

When stables have a minor virus, for example one that lasts no more than two or three months, the horses often bounce back to form with a vengeance. Punters who fasten on to the winning streak can make plenty of money, particularly because the winners have poor recent form and therefore tend to start at generous prices. However, it was much more of a gradual process with Hughes's horses and there were times when the stable's luck still seemed to be out.

At the 2002 Cheltenham Festival Timbera was beaten by only a head in the National Hunt Chase, with the third horse thirteen lengths away. If the photo finish had gone the other way, it would have made a huge difference to the trainer. It was the following year before big race victory finally returned to the yard.

Hardy Eustace had in fact won the valuable Goffs Land Rover Bumper at the Fairyhouse Easter meeting, and he returned there in December to win the Royal Bond Novice Hurdle, but neither race compared with victory at Cheltenham. Fortunately Hardy Eustace continued to progress and in March he won the Royal & SunAlliance

Hurdle to bridge the twenty-one-year gap since his trainer's last success at the most important National Hunt meeting of the season.

The gelding, bought by Carlow businessman Lar Byrne for £21,000 at Goffs in June 2001 after being spotted by Hughes at his breeder's stud the previous November, was ridden by Kieran Kelly, who lost his life five months later. The twenty-five-year-old rider was the Osborne Lodge stable jockey, and he rode Balmy Native in a three-mile handicap chase at the August Friday evening meeting at Kilbeggan. Kelly had his mount in second place for much of the race, and as the runners neared the regulation fence on the final circuit he steered slightly left so that his mount would not be brought down if the leader fell.

But it was Balmy Native who fell, hitting the top of the fence. Kelly was pitched forward as the horse hit the ground with his head and his neck. In the normal course of events Kelly would have rolled clear of the horses behind and escaped unscathed. But a freak chain of events turned a normal fall into tragedy. Balmy Native's hindquarters came up because the momentum was propelling his body forwards, and they twisted round. The horse immediately behind, Central Billing ridden by Timmy Murphy, was unable to avoid bumping Balmy Native's hindquarters.

Balmy Native's front feet then struck Kelly, who was kicked again when his mount rolled over on top of him. Kelly was tended immediately by the ambulance staff, but he was in such a bad state that a local priest administered the last rites. The ambulance to Tullamore Hospital, less than ten miles away, was given a Garda escort and Kelly was then taken to the intensive care unit of Dublin's Beaumont Hospital. His head injuries proved too serious to heal, and he died four days later. At his funeral the blue and yellow colours he had worn when winning on Hardy Eustace at Cheltenham were draped over his coffin, and Hughes gave a moving tribute to his stable jockey.

Kilbeggan sees plenty of bad falls, and the casualty unit in Tullamore Hospital is frequently called upon to tend to injured jockeys, but this was the first fatality at the Midlands course since Mut Conlan lost his life fifty-one years earlier. Kelly was the first jockey to be killed on an Irish racecourse since amateur rider Jim Lombard in 1986, but less than three months after Kelly's death apprentice Seán Cleary died as a result of severe head injuries suffered in a fall at Galway. This fatality, coming so soon after that of Kelly, prompted a wholesale review of safety by the Turf Club. The deaths brought into question the effectiveness of the helmets worn by jockeys. Unlike those used by Formula One motor racing drivers, these are not moulded to the shape of the wearer's head but are made in standard sizes, all of the same shape. Several jockeys made the point that jockeys' heads come in a whole variety of different shapes.

Hardy Eustace was not the only big race winner for Hughes in the spring of 2003. Less than six weeks after that Cheltenham success, Timbera won the Irish Grand National, pipping Knock Knock on the post and making amends for his narrow defeat in the previous season's National Hunt Chase. The nine-year-old was ridden by Jim Culloty, who won three Cheltenham Gold Cups on Best Mate as well as a Grand National on Bindaree, and he was again booked for Timbera in the following season's Aintree spectacular. Surprisingly, Hughes had never had a runner in the race, but Timbera had to be scratched after developing a lung infection only days beforehand.

Just over two years later Culloty retired to start training, after repeated falls finally took their toll on his mental processes as well as his body. He admitted with remarkable candour that his nerve had been going in the weeks leading up to the Galway Festival:

Everything in the garden was rosy on the outside, but I had been mildly concussed fifteen times the previous season. Every second fall I was dazed. I was seeing double and I couldn't remember how I got to the races. That was all in the back of my mind, and I was going out for a race thinking 'I don't want to fall.' I didn't mind riding a bad jumper, but I hated riding in big fields as there is so much luck involved. You can be on the best jumper in the world, only for something to fall in front of you. The uncertainty was doing my head in. When Laragh House fell in a handicap hurdle at Killarney, the stirrup leather twisted round my ankle. The rest of the field galloped over me and I was trying to reach out to catch my horse because I didn't want him to get up and gallop off. I would be dragged along. Fortunately the leather became loose when he got up. I got to my feet and thought 'I can think of better ways of making a living than this.'

Conor O'Dwyer took over on Hardy Eustace in the 2003/04 season, but the good-topped bay gelding did not thrive on soft ground during the winter months and in his final race before Cheltenham he was narrowly beaten by Georges Girl at Gowran Park. Hughes decided to run him in the Coral Hurdle rather than go for the Champion. The latter always looked an over-ambitious target, not least because only one SunAlliance Hurdle winner had ever gone on to win the Champion Hurdle. That was Istabraq and he was exceptional. But on the Saturday evening before the festival Hughes had a change of heart.

People had been telling me that he should run in the Coral, and when people say things like that you tend to believe them. I thought he had the potential to win the Champion Hurdle from the time he started racing. I felt that Gowran Park was a track that he would hate yet he ran Georges Girl to a short head, giving her 13lb. She had gone close in the AIG Europe Champion Hurdle previously, and I thought that Hardy Eustace was as good as all those in the Champion Hurdle bar Rooster Booster. He was in great form, and I came to the conclusion that he had everything it takes to win the race if I only had the bottle to run him in it. I went through both races again before ringing the owner to tell him that I had changed my mind. But deep down I was probably the only one who thought the horse could win.

Lar Byrne had sufficient confidence in his trainer's judgement to place a number of small bets on the internet, but Hardy Eustace started at 33-1 and there had not been such a long-priced winner of the Champion Hurdle since Beech Road sprang a 50-1 shock fifteen years earlier.

When Hughes went to the weighing room to collect O'Dwyer's saddle, he was accompanied by his son, who had ridden at Cheltenham earlier in his career. Hughes was informed by O'Dwyer that there was no sign of the blinkers that Hardy Eustace was normally fitted with to concentrate his mind on the job. Richard went into the jockeys' room to look for a spare pair, but all he could find was a set with big blue luminous cups. Hughes was unhappy about using these. He hates flashy blinkers, and he had had a pair made for Hardy Eustace which had particularly small cups. He told Richard to look again while he went off to saddle the horse. Richard eventually found the right ones on Paul Carberry's peg. Carberry, who was riding Mutineer for the stable in the last race of the day, had assumed that they were for his mount.

Hughes changed the blinkers when the horses were in the parade ring, and the bell rang for the jockeys to mount before he had a chance to discuss tactics with O'Dwyer. As he legged his jockey into the saddle, Hughes said: 'You know the horse well enough. Do your best and make plenty of use of him.'

What he had said nagged Hughes as he made his way through the packed crowds to the stands. He was worried that O'Dwyer would go too fast and that the horse would not last home up the final hill. He also knew from his riding days that the last thing a jockey is told is what he remembers best. He turned to Richard and asked him to get to O'Dwyer. 'Tell him not to go mad. This horse has as much foot as any of them.'

Hughes junior eased his way through the crowds before vaulting over the rails and running up the course to where the runners were turning to canter back past the stands. The instructions were duly relayed, and followed to the letter, Hardy Eustace's already proven stamina proving the decisive factor when Richard Johnson on Rooster Booster threw down the gauntlet at the final flight.

> Conor rode the perfect race. Hardy Eustace made ground at almost every hurdle, and all the way I thought he would win. He met the second last hurdle wrong but came back under Conor when he landed. In the winner's enclosure, the press asked me if this was better than winning the race on Monksfield. I replied that it was so long ago that I couldn't remember, but deep down I knew that it was better because I had put so much work into getting the horse there. Also I had gone for so long when I couldn't train my horses properly, and in those days any thoughts of winning a Champion Hurdle were out of the question. It was a huge boost.

Those who considered Hardy Eustace's win a fluke were made to think again when the gelding confirmed at Punchestown the form he had shown against Rooster Booster. In the 2005 Champion Hurdle the Hughes-trained gelding did it again, once more leading from start to finish, this time staying on too strongly for Harchibald, who had looked a certainty jumping the final flight, and Brave Inca. He attempted to do it again in 2006, but his chances of becoming the sixth horse to win the race three times were dealt a severe blow when his preparation was interrupted by a bug. He managed only third behind Brave Inca, and he was almost certainly past his best when he came fourth to surprise winner Sublimity twelve months later. But his trainer had already joined Fred Rimell and Fred Winter as the only men to have won the Champion Hurdle as both a jockey and a trainer.

BIGGEST RACES WON

1981
Irish Lincolnshire   Dellersbeck

1982
Supreme Novices' Hurdle   Miller Hill

1985
Galway Plate   Chow Mein

2003
Royal & SunAlliance Hurdle   Hardy Eustace
Irish Grand National   Timbera

2004
Champion Hurdle   Hardy Eustace
Emo Oil Champion Hurdle   Hardy Eustace

2005
Champion Hurdle   Hardy Eustace
Pertemps Final   Oulart

2007
AIG Europe Champion Hurdle   Hardy Eustace

6

JOHN OXX

Longchamp, 1 October 2000. The Prix de l'Arc de Triomphe. The mighty Sinndar is opposed in the market by last year's winner Montjeu who starts at 5-4 on, but it is the Aga Khan's horse who is driven into the lead on the final turn. He sweeps past his pacemaker, and he is ridden out all the way to the line to become the first Irish-trained winner for twenty-two years of what many regard as Europe's greatest race.

John Oxx's career may have got off to a shaky start but it steadily blossomed, and he succeeded in attracting patronage from both the Aga Khan and Sheikh Mohammed. He now trains some of the best-bred horses in Europe, and he has turned out a succession of high-class performers. Top of the list is Sinndar, who swept almost all before him in 2000 when his triumphs included the Derby as well as the Prix de l'Arc de Triomphe. There have been many other Group One winners and their trainer is widely recognised as a major player. He has also made a formidable contribution to racing with a lengthy stint as chairman of the Irish Racehorse Trainers' Association.

His father had been training for seven years, and was already well established, when John Mortimer Oxx was born on 14 July 1950. John Oxx senior owned the Currabeg yard on the Kildare side of The Curragh where he successfully prepared the winners of eight Irish classics, including Arctic Storm, who went some way towards making amends for an unlucky defeat in the first running of the Irish Sweeps Derby by winning the 1962 Champion Stakes.

Oxx junior never expected to do anything other than train horses, and his father had the same expectations for his only son, making sure that he spent most of his teenage school holidays assisting in the yard. After leaving school, Oxx spent five years at University College, Dublin qualifying as a vet – 'but even then everyone looked upon me as my father's assistant and, for my part, I never had any intention of practising'.

His knowledge of training came solely from his father; while he did have a look at the racing scene in Australia, it was not much more than an extended holiday. He had been working as a full-time assistant trainer for some six years when his father retired at the end of 1978, shortly before his sixty-ninth birthday, and switched roles to become assistant to his son. 'We had minor disagreements, almost on a daily basis, but he was an easy man to get on with – and he was always willing to stand in for me if I couldn't go to a particular meeting.'

His father's experience and support were particularly helpful when things started to go wrong. Oxx took over a string of seventy well-bred horses, all Flat racers, and sent out twenty-seven winners in his first season. It was a satisfactory if far from spectacular beginning, but after a further forty winners in 1980 people began to take note of the new man at the helm at Currabeg. He was sent more horses, but a big increase in the number of two-year-olds in 1981 brought some unwelcome problems. 'I didn't realise it at the time, but having a lot of two-year-olds puts you in a high-risk position. They are like kids in their first year at school. They pick up everything going, and they are the ones who start off any virus infections.'

The winners slumped to a meagre fifteen that year, and stable jockey Ray Carroll decided to accept an offer to join Adrian Maxwell at South Lodge near Nine Mile House in County Tipperary. Oxx approached Pat Eddery, who was in his second season as stable jockey to Vincent O'Brien. Eddery agreed to ride anything Oxx thought had a chance of winning, whenever he was in Ireland and whenever Ballydoyle had no runner. Eddery, who had effectively kissed goodbye to his run of British championships when he accepted the O'Brien job, was keen to have a full book of rides at Irish meetings. He also found Oxx's professional, yet undemanding manner much to his liking ('John is a lovely man, a real gentleman') and the association clicked almost immediately. Eddery's brilliance often made the difference between defeat and victory, and as Oxx's horses tended to operate on a lower plane than those at Ballydoyle, the jockey was normally available for the Currabeg rides. The stable's winners steadily climbed back up to a respectable total and in 1986 Oxx reached the half-century for the first time. Fifty winners might not seem a lot today but there was less racing in those days, and that year only Dermot Weld sent out more.

When Cash Asmussen replaced Eddery as the Ballydoyle stable jockey in 1987, Oxx made a similar arrangement with the tall Texan. Asmussen came in for plenty of criticism from Irish racegoers, many of whom were singularly unimpressed with his style of riding; Asmussen often seemed to leave his effort too late and to be too easy on his mounts. However, Oxx was a supporter:

Cash had a very quiet style and, rather like Bill Williamson who used to ride for my father, he was always flat to the boards before he reached for his stick. If you studied the videos, you would see that he was using his whip even though, from the stands, it looked as if he wasn't. The reason is that he swung it low, unlike Eddery and others who brought their arm right up.

It was Asmussen who rode Oxx's first classic winner, Eurobird, in the 1987 Irish St Leger. Forty-four years earlier Oxx's father had scored his first classic success in the same race, with Solferino. The father–son connection did not end there, because Eurobird carried the same colours, those of Belfast businessman Gerald Jennings, as Sorbus, who in 1978 finished runner-up in the Irish 1,000 Guineas, the Yorkshire Oaks and the Irish St Leger, and who was first past the post in the Irish Oaks but was controversially put back to second for causing interference to Fair Salinia. Oxx senior, who trained the luckless filly, always maintained that he was robbed. He was not the only one: Sorbus having come home a comfortable winner, the crowd around the weighing room gave a hostile reception to the result of the stewards' inquiry, and the presentation of the trophy to Fair Salinia's connections was greeted with stony silence.

Eurobird's Irish St Leger win (the stable won the race again with Petite Ile two years later and with Kastoria in 2006) should have been the first leg of a notable double for Oxx and Asmussen because Excellenza ran out an easy winner of the Irish Cesarewitch thirty-five minutes later. However, she had been declared with blinkers and ran without them. Oxx, on cloud nine after his first classic success, had failed to notice the missing blinkers when the filly left the parade ring, while Asmussen, who had never ridden her before, was not even aware that she was meant to wear them. The stewards deliberated long and hard – none of them could recall a similar case, and they were not sure what action they should take, if any – before ruling that Excellenza should be disqualified.

Oxx had first been sent horses by Sheikh Mohammed in 1986, and the association got off to a flying start when the first runner in the Dubai prince's maroon and white colours won at Naas. This was Master Swordsman, a cast-off from Luca Cumani's stable, and the following year Sheikh Mohammed showed his appreciation of this initial success by increasing his numbers with Oxx to seventeen. During the winter of 1987/88 Oxx considered his riding options for the following season. Vincent O'Brien had decided against renewing Asmussen's contract and had appointed John Reid as his replacement. Oxx could probably have made the same arrangement with the new man at Ballydoyle as he had done with Eddery and Asmussen, but he had more than enough quality horses to warrant employing a top-class stable jockey of his own. All the leading Irish riders were already employed by rival trainers. Tempting them away would be costly, and Oxx had no wish to cause any aggravation. He turned to Australia, as his father had done before him, and the rider he picked was Ron Quinton.

Quinton, then aged forty, had been eight times champion jockey in New South Wales, had ridden nearly 2,000 winners and had spent a month the previous season riding in England for Geoff Lewis and Barry Hills. He would have gone back to Britain had he been offered a stable jockey job, so, despite never having been to Ireland or met Oxx, he was willing to travel. He agreed to come for a year, and he stayed for three.

The new association had their first Group One success when Flamenco Wave won the Moyglare Stud Stakes at The Curragh in September 1988. That victory was also Oxx's first really major win for Sheikh Mohammed, who tended to keep his best stock for his trainers in Britain, although he steadily increased the numbers he had at Currabeg. In 1990, for example, he owned forty-five of the stable's horses and in 1998, when Oxx was training nearly 150 horses, fifty of them belonged to Sheikh Mohammed.

By that stage Oxx was also training fifty for the Aga Khan who first sent horses to Currabeg in 1989. The Aga, and his ancestors, had long bred horses in Ireland but the fifteen two-year-olds he sent to Oxx that year were the first that he had trained in the country. Having lost Shergar, the best horse he ever owned, to a sensational kidnapping on the part of a dissident IRA group six years earlier, his decision to support Irish racing was widely regarded as a considerable act of faith in both the sport and in Ireland itself.

The Aga Khan had confessed to having 'absolutely no interest in bloodstock' when in 1960 he took over the family studs following the death of his father, Prince Aly Khan, in a car crash. Indeed he reduced the broodmare numbers from ninety to fifty, although this was partly a consequence of the heavy death duties payable on his father's death, and on that of the third Aga Khan three years earlier. He also concentrated his breeding empire in France. 'My first priority was obviously the figures, the second was to look at the people I was working with, and the third was to learn about the families and the breeding principles, and look at the way the farms were being run.'

The Aga proved not just to be a fast learner but to have an aptitude for bloodstock breeding that few people possess. He shrewdly bought the bloodstock empires of Marcel Boussac and fellow owner-breeder Mme François Dupré, weeded out the non-essential mares and concentrated on producing well-bred foals that turned into sound, tough racehorses of an exceptionally high overall standard. He later became a generous benefactor to racing and provided the impetus, as well as considerable funding, for the redevelopment of Chantilly and The Curragh racecourses. His reputation as a breeder was sky high by the time he first sent horses to Oxx.

In 1990 the Aga Khan sent a further batch of two-year-olds to Currabeg, and he was rewarded with twenty winners in Ireland that season. However, the following year the numbers increased to a level that many of Oxx's rival trainers, and some members of the media, regarded as alarming. The reason was a dispute with the Jockey Club in Britain.

In 1989 the Aga's Aliysa ran out an emphatic winner of the Oaks, but a derivative of the prohibited substance camphor was found in her urine sample, and she seemed certain to be disqualified. The Jockey Club prevaricated, but in December that year the filly's owner-breeder resigned his honorary membership. He was reported as saying that he was 'making a stand for everyone whose horse has suffered disqualification due to an unexplainable positive test in which camphor played a part'. He insisted that Aliysa had been in total isolation for seventy-two hours before the Oaks and that he could not therefore understand how she could have come into contact with camphor during that period.

Aliysa was not finally disqualified until 20 November 1990, nearly eighteen months after the race. A fortnight later the Aga Khan announced that his horses in training in Britain (numbering around ninety) would be removed, and that he would not have another runner in the country until the scientific management of racing there had reached a standard he considered acceptable. The result was a substantial increase in the numbers he had in training in France and Ireland, where John Oxx felt compelled to raid even the modest minor courses in order to find winning opportunities for his principal patron's horses.

Not surprisingly, the trainer found himself at the centre of controversy. Small trainers, and their owners, were up in arms at suddenly having to contend with the Aga Khan's expensively bred horses. Oxx insisted that the Aga was entitled to run his horses at any course in the country, but his patron's approach was markedly different to that of the only other owner (Sheikh Mohammed apart) with an equally large number of horses in Ireland. This was the Moyglare Stud Farm, owned by Swiss-based multi-millionaire Walter Haefner and managed by Stan Cosgrove. They instructed Dermot Weld that he was not to run any of the sixty or so horses he trained for them at minor Irish courses, and they drew up a list of the tracks on the no-go list to ensure there could be no misunderstanding.

However, after a couple of seasons the controversy petered out as the Aga Khan's runners became an accepted fact of racing life in Ireland. Indeed, many racegoers in outlying parts of the country appreciated seeing such well-bred horses, and in any case the total number of runners from the Oxx stable was less than that of its principal rivals. In 1993, for example, he had 327 runners, compared with 550 for Dermot Weld and 520 for Jim Bolger. In that same year Oxx ran 99 different horses (57 belonging to the Aga Khan), whereas Weld ran 133 and Bolger 129.

One of the reasons that Oxx tends to have fewer runners is that many of his two-year-olds never see a racecourse. He adopts an ultra-patient policy, and he is often quite happy for his horses not to make their debuts until they are three. 'I don't really have two-year-old types – most of mine are bred to take a bit of time.'

A notable exception was Manntari, who won the 1993 National Stakes by ten lengths, twice as far as any winner of Ireland's most important two-year-old race since Santa Claus thirty years earlier. Unfortunately Manntari proved no Santa Claus (who went on to win the Irish 2,000 Guineas, the Derby and the Irish Derby in spectacular style) and finished last in the Irish 2,000 Guineas. He did not race again, and he was sold to stand at stud in New Zealand.

Unusually for an Irish trainer, Oxx has never run horses over jumps, not even to give the yard an interest during the winter months. He once got as far as running a gelding in bumpers, to help his sister who bred the horse, but that was all. However, he has gone out of his way to assist the racing and breeding industries. During his long period as chairman of the Irish Racehorse Trainers' Association he pushed hard for the advancement of his fellow trainers, and National Hunt trainers received just as much support as their Flat counterparts. He also served as chairman of the Irish National Stud.

When I was asked in July 1985 by the then Minister for Agriculture to take over the National Stud post, I said to myself 'I'm working round the clock as it is, and it's not as if I don't have enough commitments already', but I felt it was an honour to be asked and I considered it my duty to accept. I took on the chairmanship of the Trainers' Association because nobody else would, but I believe in the Association. It's important.

However, there was never any bombast, or attempt to pull rank, in either post. Oxx is an essentially modest man who puts his points across with reasoned argument, and he goes out of his way to listen and understand opposing schools of thought. This modesty extends to his way of life and to the cars he drives. Most Flat trainers regard a Mercedes as a badge of office, as essential as an all-weather gallop. Not Oxx. For many years he preferred a Toyota Carina, and it was nothing to see him driving the same one for five years or more.

One of Oxx's most colourful owners is Sean Coughlan. Brought up within a stone's throw of The Curragh, Coughlan left school at fourteen to work in a local cutlery factory for the equivalent of 50p a week. Two years later he followed his father into the Irish Army, but when he was still a private six years later he moved to London and got a job on the buses. He is fond of relating how he arrived in the capital 'with a packet of cigarettes in one pocket and nothing in the other'. He was a conductor and then a driver before he realised that he could earn three times as much working on a building site. In 1959, when he was twenty-six, he began doing extra work in his spare time and this fast-developing sideline became J.J. Coughlan Ltd, a construction company based in the South London suburb of Perry Vale. He was proud of operating on the principle that 'if I found anyone who knew more about the building trade than I did, I gave them a job and I paid them enough to make sure they stayed'.

By the time he and his wife Anne moved back to The Curragh, the company had a workforce of 150 and the couple had become hooked on racing. Their first horse was Joshua's Daughter, who injured herself so badly soon after her purchase that the vet recommended putting her down. Coughlan insisted that she be saved for breeding, and she rewarded her new owners by producing Ben's Pearl, winner of the 1988 Irish Cambridgeshire when trained by Oxx.

Coughlan also had horses in Britain with David Elsworth, including the first horse he bred, Sovereign Paul, who owed his name to his owner's audience with the Pope. Coughlan was so impressed that he not only named the horse after the Vatican's principal resident, but changed his racing colours from the green, white and orange of Ireland to the Pope's white and yellow with red on the cap.

Elsworth was rather less impressed with Sovereign Paul. He eventually informed the horse's owner-breeder that the gelding was no good and would never win a race. Coughlan transferred him to Jimmy Fox, who sent the horse to Bath to beat one of Elsworth's in a photo-finish. Coughlan has a framed picture of the horse in the Bath winner's enclosure, with a caption saying 'Where's Ellsie now?'

The best horse that Elsworth trained for Coughlan was Indian Ridge, who won the Jersey Stakes in 1988 and the King's Stand Stakes twelve months later. Immediately after the former victory, Coughlan threw his arms round the trainer and hugged him so tight that the seat of his trousers somehow became torn. Fellow trainer Paul Kelleway, noticing the sorry state of the Elsworth morning suit, remarked: 'God, Ellsie. I hate to think what would happen if you won the Derby for that fellow!'

Coughlan sent Ben's Pearl to be covered by Indian Ridge in 1990, and again in 1991, but she died of a heart attack the following year. However, her two progeny were both high class, Ridgewood Ben winning the 1994 Gladness Stakes and Ridgewood Pearl proving the outstanding filly of her generation in 1995.

Coughlan has long rated that Gladness victory as one of the best moments of his racing life: 'Vincent O'Brien's College Chapel started odds-on and I thought we hadn't a hope, yet my home-bred colt ran away with the race. The fact that it was at The Curragh, where I was brought up, made it extra special.' Coughlan has tended to celebrate victories by throwing a party at the Cill Dara Golf Club ('I like to make the best of it and I also like to see everybody having a bit of fun') and there were several during the incredible year of Ridgewood Pearl. She won the Irish 1,000 Guineas, the Coronation Stakes at Royal Ascot, the Prix du Moulin at Longchamp and the Breeders' Cup Mile in New York.

Her only defeat that season came in the Queen Elizabeth II Stakes when Willie Carson stole a march on his rivals with a brilliant and audacious tactical manoeuvre. The ground at Ascot that day was officially good, with good to soft patches. The wily Carson spotted that the ground on the far rails was fast, if not actually firm, because it had been protected from rain and watering by overhanging tree branches. He made straight for this on Bahri, and he kept his mount there until he neared the final turn. Carson would have been vilified by the press had his mount been beaten, but Bahri gained such an advantage that he was able to storm past the post six lengths clear of Ridgewood Pearl.

The Breeders' Cup Mile put the gloss back on Ridgewood Pearl's season, and she then won the Cartier Horse of the Year Award. Her delighted owners responded by commissioning a statue of their filly and presenting it to The Curragh racecourse.

Although 1995 was the year of Ridgewood Pearl so far as John Oxx was concerned, he also won that season's Prix de l'Opera with Timarida, who won all but one of her eight starts that year and added three more Group One victories the following season. This daughter of Kalaglow was owned and bred by the Aga Khan, who despite making the mistake of selling the dam for a mere 5,200 guineas in 1994, struck gold with the mare Ebaziya. Her first three foals all won Group One races – Ebadiyla the 1997 Irish Oaks and French St Leger, Edabiya the following year's Moyglare Stud Stakes and Enzeli the 1999 Ascot Gold Cup. They were all trained by Oxx, who also handled Ebaziya.

Less than three months after Enzeli's Gold Cup win, Sinndar won the National Stakes. It wasn't an impressive win – he was being ridden along before the straight – and it was not until the bay colt, with a white star on his forehead and another above his nostrils, made an encouraging reappearance in the Ballysax Stakes at Leopardstown the following April that Oxx really felt that he had a Derby horse on his hands. He had never had a runner in the Derby before but Sinndar, given a faultless ride by Johnny Murtagh, raced in a perfect position and forged ahead in the final furlong to become the first Irish-trained winner of the Blue Riband since Secreto sixteen years earlier. The son of Grand Lodge was the first Derby winner to be trained on The Curragh since Santa Claus, and this was the first year since 1958 that Irish trainers had won both the Derby and the Grand National, Ted Walsh having been successful at Aintree with Papillon. Oxx is a calm and normally unruffled individual but winning the great race made a huge impact.

> The Epsom Derby is the most historic race, and it's a carved-in-stone type result. I often dreamed of winning it but it was not something I thought could happen. The whole day was something of a whirl, and at the time it didn't really sink in. At midnight, after I had played the video twice, I finally realised I had won the Derby. And, after a day like that, I found it hard to sleep but the dream had come true.

Oxx's wife, Catriona, revealed just how much Sinndar's win meant to her husband: 'People think that John is cool and quiet about everything, but that's because he is a bit shy. He's not really like that and, at the back of it all, he was as excited as anybody. He was also very, very happy. Winning the Derby is the ultimate dream in racing.'

Winning the Irish Derby can mean just as much to an Irish trainer, and at Currabeg there were special reasons for wanting to complete the Epsom–Curragh double with Sinndar.

> I have vivid memories of the 1962 Irish Derby, and what the result meant in our house. Arctic Storm was an unlucky loser because he was brought to his knees at the top of the hill, and he was only beaten a short head. My father was proud of his horse but he was disappointed because Arctic Storm could have done so much better. He would have been a worthy Irish Derby winner, and he was a better horse than Tambourine II who did nothing subsequently.

Sinndar, surprisingly, was the first Derby winner to run in the Irish equivalent for seven years. He was opposed at The Curragh by the

Michael Jarvis-trained Holding Court – who had run away with the French Derby – and by Sir Michael Stoute's 2,000 Guineas winner King's Best. Oxx's colt started favourite but his trainer had serious concerns both before the race and during it:

> On the previous morning Sinndar came in lame from exercise. He had a sore heel that was stinging him badly. There was a little bit of filling in his pastern and we had to work on it overnight. Nobody knew anything about this, but watching the race from my usual seat in the stands I was worried when I saw him being niggled along. I still don't know for sure but I think he lost his concentration. He used to start going home from that part of The Curragh, but it was possibly also that the sore heel was annoying him. He was a very lazy worker on the gallops but he had always travelled very well in his races.

Fortunately Sinndar kept responding to Johnny Murtagh's urgings to lead early in the straight and he came home nine lengths clear. His task was made a lot easier when Holding Court failed to fire, while King's Best fractured his off-fore cannon bone and was pulled up. Sinndar was not a particularly big horse and the fact that he was so well balanced probably made him look smaller than he was. However, in full flow he was a real machine, and he collected a million-dollar millennium bonus for his owner from race sponsor Budweiser for completing the Derby double.

Oxx then aimed his colt at the Prix de l'Arc de Triomphe. In 2000, the big French race, the most important middle-distance event in Europe, attracted only ten runners, the smallest field since 1946, with Sinndar and Montjeu frightening off many would-be contenders. Montjeu failed to reproduce the form of his win the previous year, and Sinndar crowned a wonderful season by clocking the second-fastest time in the history of the race. It was a notable day for Oxx, who also won the Prix de l'Abbaye with Namid, while Murtagh completed a Group One treble on Petrushka in the Prix de l'Opera.

It means everything to have a horse like Sinndar. Every trainer hopes to get the top one some day and most never get the chance. It's not certain that it's going to happen, and you can't plan it unless you are operating at the level of Ballydoyle. You just feel grateful that a horse like him has come along, and when it turns out so well you get a lot of satisfaction. You probably get a little more relaxed as a result, but it doesn't make you any less ambitious or work any less hard.

There is always pressure, which comes from myself, not from my clients. You work hard to get results, and you feel disappointment when you don't get them or get them good enough. However, as time goes by and you grow older, you tend to be more philosophical. Training racehorses can be bloody hard work, but if you feel confident that you are working as hard as you can and you are doing your best, then the results will come. You never sit still. Every year I am looking at the business, trying to improve it in some way. The principles never change, and the routine is basically the same, but there are always little things that I try to improve. If you sit still in this game, and say you know it all and are doing everything right, then you will go backwards.

Similar words of wisdom are often dispensed in the winner's enclosure, much to the delight of the press who know that whenever there is an Oxx winner they are assured of good copy. Bespectacled and almost bald, he has the air of a university professor, but few academics are capable of so interesting and entertaining their audiences. Had John Oxx elected to train students rather than race-horses, his lectures would be delivered to full houses. Furthermore, he gives every impression of being easy-going, friendly and relaxed, although he points out that the winner's enclosure, a place predomi-nantly of achievement and satisfaction, can give a false impression.

Three years after Sinndar, Oxx had a second Irish Derby winner in Alamshar. This colt, only third at Epsom, was not expected to prove any match for the Aga Khan's other runner. Dalakhani, trained by

Alain de Royer-Dupré and a comfortable winner of the French Derby, started at 7-4 on, while Alamshar (4-1) carried the green and chocolate-hooped colours made famous by the owner's grandfather, but now used for second strings. However, the favourite's rider, Christophe Soumillon, had never ridden at The Curragh until the previous day, and his inexperience resulted in him heading for home the minute he turned into the straight. The final three furlongs at The Curragh are uphill all the way, and local jockeys are normally reluctant to commit their horses so early unless they are riding out-and-out stayers. Furthermore, Dalakhani's greatest asset was his turn of foot. Johnny Murtagh launched his challenge, and Alamshar wore down his opponent to win by a hard-fought half a length.

The winner was already suffering from muscle problems in his back. Dr Marc Baudoux, a noted French chiropractor, had been flown over to treat him two days before the race, but the problems reappeared repeatedly and Liz Kent, the Irish equine physiotherapist, became a regular visitor to Currabeg. She ensured that the colt was fit for the King George VI and Queen Elizabeth Diamond Stakes the following month, and he ran out an easy winner. Murtagh was again at his tactical best, seizing the advantage on the final turn and kicking clear.

Murtagh had been with Oxx for most of his career, taking over as stable jockey when Ron Quinton went back to Australia, but a constant battle with the scales forced him to go to extraordinary lengths, often running for miles day after day in warm clothes, grimly sweating off the pounds. On occasion even this did not work. When he hurt his back in a fall from a two-year-old at Royal Ascot, he had to suspend the weight-reducing runs. He decided to take a break from riding when he found himself unable to ride at 8st 11lb in August 2003, and that October he elected to end his season early. Mick Kinane, finding that his Ballydoyle contract was not going to be renewed, had discussions with Oxx. The trainer asked Murtagh for a commitment that he would be able to ride at a reasonable weight the following season and, when Murtagh said he was unable to give such an undertaking, Kinane was appointed first jockey at Currabeg.

The pair cemented their partnership the following June when Azamour won the St James's Palace Stakes, but this colt might well have won the Derby had his trainer adopted a more adventurous policy. He had sufficient stamina to win the Beresford Stakes over a mile as a two-year-old, as Alamshar had done the previous season, and the way he stayed on strongly, from quite some way back, to finish third in the 2,000 Guineas suggested he needed further. His running in the Irish equivalent, outpaced when the gallop suddenly quickened, also indicated that this was a colt who was going to be better beyond a mile, and he was in the Derby.

The problem was that he was by Night Shift, whose progeny have tended to be best at no more than a mile. In The Groove and Daryaba, both Group One winners over a mile and a half, were notable exceptions, but Oxx decided to play safe and go for the Royal Ascot mile race instead. However, the signs were there for all to see when Azamour needed every yard of ten furlongs to win the Irish Champion Stakes at Leopardstown in September. Oxx then decided to prepare him for a tilt at the King George VI and Queen Elizabeth Diamond Stakes the following season, and Kinane's mount won that race rather more easily than any of his previous Group One successes.

The 2004 Derby, won by North Light, had not in retrospect taken a lot of winning and it is hard to escape the conclusion that Azamour would have proved too good for that colt had he been sent to Epsom. However, Oxx's conservatism was to be rewarding for the Aga Khan. Proving his ability to win at the very top level at a mile, ten furlongs, and a mile and a half meant that Azamour retired to stud a more valuable horse than if he had merely won the Derby!

BIGGEST RACES WON

1987

Irish St Leger	Eurobird

1988

Moyglare Stud Stakes	Flamenco Wave

1989

Irish St Leger	Petite Ile

1993

National Stakes	Manntari

1995

Irish 1,000 Guineas	Ridgewood Pearl
Coronation Stakes	Ridgewood Pearl
Prix du Moulin	Ridgewood Pearl
Breeders' Cup Mile	Ridgewood Pearl

1996

Yorkshire Oaks	Key Change
Preis-Bayerisches Zuchtrennen	Timarida
Irish Champion Stakes	Timarida
Beverly D. Stakes	Timarida

1997

Irish Oaks	Ebadiyla
French St Leger	Ebadiyla

1998

Irish Oaks	Winona
Moyglare Stud Stakes	Edabiya

1999
Ascot Gold Cup   Enzeli
National Stakes   Sinndar

2000
Derby   Sinndar
Irish Derby   Sinndar
Prix de l'Arc de Triomphe   Sinndar
Prix de l'Abbaye   Namid

2003
Irish Derby   Alamshar
King George VI and Queen Elizabeth
    Diamond Stakes   Alamshar

2004
St James's Palace Stakes   Azamour
Irish Champion Stakes   Azamour

2005
Prince of Wales Stakes   Azamour
King George VI and Queen Elizabeth
    Diamond Stakes   Azamour

2006
Irish St Leger   Kastoria

7

MICHAEL O'BRIEN

Champion jockey in the States . . . a spine-breaking fall . . . paralysis . . . training from a wheelchair. Michael O'Brien's story provides a frightening example of the dangers of racing and, at the same time, it serves as an inspiration to the disabled everywhere.

Born on 13 March 1943, O'Brien was brought up in the Dublin suburb of Newcastle, which in the 1940s and 1950s was a small village separated from Dublin by acres of green fields. His father, who had no particular interest in racing, travelled into the capital each day to the Cadbury's chocolate factory where he worked as a boilerman. Michael's older brother Leo, intending when he left school at fourteen to become a farm labourer, walked a few miles up the road to Rathcoole to ask Tom Taaffe (father of the legendary Pat and grandfather of Cheltenham Gold Cup-winning trainer Tom) for a job. He was told that there were no vacancies on the farm, but there was one in Taaffe's training stable.

Leo O'Brien slowly progressed from mucking out the boxes to exercising the horses. As the string returned home one day in September 1956, stable jockey Toss Taaffe (Pat's brother) told young O'Brien that he would be riding at The Curragh the following week. 'You mean as a jockey?' the boy replied. 'Holy cow.'

O'Brien was frightened silly. He had no intention of becoming a jockey. His ambitions consisted of nothing more than earning a few pounds so that he could go out in the evenings and enjoy himself. But he finished third on that first ride, on a filly called Similar. When she returned to The Curragh six weeks later O'Brien again had the mount, and this time she won. Most of the Taaffe horses were jumpers, but O'Brien began to get more and more rides on the Flat horses. As he grew older and heavier, he was given mounts on some of the National Hunt runners.

Younger brother Michael was impressed, but when he left school at sixteen there were no jobs going in the Taaffe yard. Instead he went to work at The Curragh for John Oxx senior. However, he soon realised that he needed to go elsewhere. He was required to sign on as an apprentice for four years, and he knew he was too heavy to make any progress on the Flat. He could see himself spending all that time mucking out stables, with riding restricted to exercise work. He pressed Leo about a job in a jumping yard. Leo again spoke to Tom Taaffe and this time the trainer agreed to take him on. However, he rode only five winners in eight years, and at the age of twenty-five he decided to move to America.

Leo was already there. One Saturday morning one of the lads in Taaffe's yard had pointed out an advertisement in *The Irish Field*: a top jumping stable in the States wanted two jockeys. Leo got his sister to write the application letter, but when the reply came back with a pile of forms to be filled in, he lost interest. In any case, he had no real wish to go to America. He was happy where he was, and with his life at Taaffe's stable. However, bloodstock agent Tom Cooper spoke to him at the races ten days later, and told the bemused O'Brien that Raymond Guest was flying to Dublin the following week and was going to interview him.

Guest was the American ambassador to Ireland when he won the 1968 Derby with Sir Ivor, and his L'Escargot was later to win two Cheltenham Gold Cups as well as the 1975 Grand National. O'Brien went into Dublin to meet the American, albeit with some reluctance.

He still did not want to go, but at the end of the interview he was told that his flight was booked.

He became an instant success in the States, and won on his first five rides. American jump racing is small by comparison with that in England and Ireland, but O'Brien quickly reached the top level. Soon he was riding for most of the leading trainers with the exception of Jonathan Sheppard.

Sheppard, still in his twenties, was an Englishman educated at Eton. He had been brought up in racing, and he wanted to train in his native country. The problem was that his father, Dan, was a handicapper and the Jockey Club would not grant him a licence to train while Sheppard senior held office. He therefore moved to the USA, where he set about building up the best jumping stable in the country.

Leo told Sheppard about his brother, and Michael O'Brien left Ireland to work for the expatriate Englishman. The job promised rides, although it had been made clear to O'Brien that there were others higher up the pecking order.

I had a few rides in that first year, but I was only about fourth in line and I didn't get on that well. The following year things started to click. The first jockey was a greedy kind of guy, and he wanted to ride the best horses in each race. He would get off Sheppard's horses to ride others that he thought had a better chance. I won on one of his rejects, and it was the first Graded stakes race that Sheppard had ever won. He began to think that, instead of messing about with yer man, he could put me up and the horses would still win. Then, in the spring, the stable jockey broke his collar-bone. I rode most of the runners and had a good few winners. About eighteen months after I went out there, I was made stable jockey.

In 1972, another two and a half years later, O'Brien became champion jockey. He is modest about the achievement. 'I had the best job in American jump racing. Sheppard had most of the best horses, and whoever rode for him would have been champion.'

O'Brien missed some of the key races the following year through injury – he broke his shoulder, his collar-bone and part of his hand – but he was on the crest of a wave by the time it came to the Carolina Cup at Camden on 30 March 1974. The race came just seventeen days after his thirty-first birthday, his wife Ann was pregnant with daughter Ann-Marie (who was later to play a key role as her father's assistant trainer), and he was riding Athenian Idol. The six-year-old was the best in the States and was the 1973 steeplechaser of the year. However, as he jumped the second fence, he suffered a massive heart attack. O'Brien was hurled clear as the horse crashed to the ground, but was struck in the chest by the hoof of one of the other horses. The kick was delivered with the force of a piledriver. He was also struck in the face, and the impact broke his nose. Knocked unconscious, he came round as he was being loaded into the ambulance.

He realised almost immediately that he had a number of injuries and that something was seriously damaged. Indeed, he was so badly hurt that he had difficulty talking. That night it was the doctors who talked to him. They explained that he was paralysed from the chest down and that he would never be able to walk again.

It didn't really sink in. I thought they had probably not diagnosed it correctly, and I had a lot else wrong with me to worry about. When the spinal cord is cut, they normally operate immediately to relieve the pressure. They couldn't do that in this case. I was so badly injured, they feared I would not survive the operation. Also I wasn't in any great shape to have an operation. In the spring it used to take me a long time to get down to a proper riding weight, and I had been doing a lot of wasting for that meeting.

When a blood clot moved from one of his legs to his lungs, O'Brien nearly died. After six weeks in hospital, one of them in intensive care because of the blood clot, he was moved to the hospital at the University of Pennsylvania where the inevitable depression finally set in. His despair can be imagined. He had been struck down in his prime, he had a wife to support and soon a child too, and he had no means of earning an income. He had been harshly, and unfairly, condemned to spending the rest of his life in a wheelchair. How could it have happened to him? It didn't seem possible, yet the evidence all round him – doctors, nurses and carers – told him with stark and horrifying clarity that this was no mere nightmare.

One of the main reasons that the patient had been sent to the University of Pennsylvania was because the faculty had a special counselling service, including resident psychiatrists, to treat not just the disabled but their families as well. They also prepared the paralysed for a new life, usually involving an office job. 'The guys that counsel you, the psychiatrists and the others, make you look forward rather than back to what your life was. They seemed to know what buttons to press. They only needed to press one with me.'

O'Brien was made to realise that he had great talent with horses and that, while he could no longer ride them, there was nothing to stop him from training them. He was unable to start straight away – he had to have further medical care and accustom his paralysed body to the wheelchair – but some of the Americans he had been riding for agreed to back him in his new venture. And once again Leo was there when he needed him. On this occasion, though, Michael's elder brother was also battling with adversity. He had struck up a profitable partnership with Gran Khan, who replaced Athenian Idol as the top jump horse, but at Monmouth Park in New Jersey a bad fall ended his riding career. He was paralysed, fortunately only for a short time, but he broke his jaw and fractured his skull, and there were unpleasant after-effects. 'The injuries left me dopey, and it was a year before I really recovered. For a lot of that time I couldn't see, and often I couldn't hear either.'

The two battered brothers discussed their plans for the future.

Michael decided that it should be in Ireland rather than America. Ann felt she needed her family round her, particularly with a small child as well as a paralysed husband to care for. It was agreed that Michael, rather than his elder brother, should be the trainer and Leo his assistant.

One of the pair's top priorities when they returned to Ireland was to find a stable yard that was reasonably flat and that did not have any narrow passages or steps between the boxes. Such problems are a feature of many of the older yards, and so Michael decided to buy land on The Curragh at Rathbride, not far from the racecourse. The brothers built a yard that was wheelchair-friendly and set up shop with twelve horses. Michael bought a house in Naas some ten miles away, travelling everywhere in a van so that he could take the wheelchair with him.

The winners were not slow in coming, and Bright Highway, Chorelli and Tacroy soon put their trainer on the map. On Irish Grand National day in March 1978 Bright Highway, bred by the Taaffe family and carrying the colours of American George Strawbridge, won a bumper at Fairyhouse. He was ridden by another of O'Brien's contacts from the States, Rusty Carrier. The gelding won six more races before landing the Mackeson Gold Cup at Cheltenham in November 1980. The Mackeson has lost a lot of its prestige over the years, thanks in no small part to several changes of name, but in those days it was one of the most important races of the season.

Bright Highway was only the second horse as young as six to win the race since its inaugural running in 1960, and a fortnight later he added the Hennessy Gold Cup at Newbury. He was now favourite to win the Cheltenham Gold Cup and, with 1981 being the Year of the Disabled, O'Brien's new fame seemed set to reach far beyond the racing pages. Sadly, the fickle hand of fortune struck again. In the month before the race, the horse injured a tendon above his off hind hock, and the initial prognosis was so bad that it was feared his racing days were over. Strawbridge planned to take him back to America and use him as a hunter.

Leo O'Brien decided the time had come to set up on his own. He had been overshadowed by his younger brother since their return to Ireland, and while this did not bother the unassuming Leo, he felt that his prospects would be better in America. Apart from anything else, he would not have to find the capital to build a yard, because most of the trainers in the States stable and prepare their horses on the racetracks.

He took with him the six-year-old Sports Reporter, who had won three chases off the reel before finishing third in the Galway Plate. A fast-ground performer, he won a big race on his second American start. But Leo did not find things easy. 'I had been away for nearly five years and people had forgotten me. To make a living, I had to spend most of my day riding work for other trainers. I would attend to Sports Reporter first thing in the morning, and again after I had finished with everyone else's horses.'

It was not for another two years, when his string had increased to three, that he gave up riding work for other trainers, and some years more before he was doing well enough to employ anybody. But although he still had only sixteen horses in 1991, he made racing history that year by sending Fourstars Allstar from New York to win the Irish 2,000 Guineas. This was the first time that an American-trained horse had won a European classic, and the feat has not been repeated. Leo is still training at Belmont Park and another O'Brien brother, Colm, also trains in New York.

It took Michael O'Brien little more than a season to gain compensation for the setback with Bright Highway. In the Irish Grand National at Fairyhouse on Easter Monday 1982, the Francis Flood-trained Fethard Friend was the subject of a massive plunge and was backed down to joint favouritism. However, much to the relief of the bookmakers, the O'Brien-trained King Spruce finished the stronger to beat Fethard Friend and spring a 20-1 surprise in the hands of Gerry Newman. The winner was owned by Rusty Carrier, whose talent as an amateur rider was more than matched by that of his wife Joy. She was the first woman to ride a winner of the Maryland Hunt Cup, an American steeplechase in which several of the obstacles are made of solid wooden posts and rails. Her grandmother, Mrs Miles Valentine, owned top steeplechasers on both sides of the Atlantic for several decades and ran them in colours dominated by pink hearts.

O'Brien finished 1982 as champion jumps trainer in terms of prize money. In the final month of the year he recorded a controversial one-two in the Punchestown Chase, in which he ran the previous year's winner Tacroy, Bright Highway and Chorelli. The last-named was on the comeback trail after being injured shortly before the 1979 Cheltenham Festival, and was part-owned by Charlie McCreevy. The man who was to become one of Ireland's best Ministers for Finance, as well as one of the principal architects of Irish racing's current prosperity, has been a racing fanatic ever since his schooldays when he went to the same educational establishments as Ted Walsh. He rates his association with Chorelli in that Punchestown Chase as proud a moment as any of his political achievements:

It's no secret that I like a bet, and a substantial one at that. I didn't own Chorelli as a young horse when he would have won at Cheltenham, but after he broke down he ended up being owned by Michael O'Brien, Aidan Walsh and myself. Stable jockey Gerry Newman rode Bright Highway at Punchestown even though the horse had been off for over two years. Frank Berry was on Tacroy, and the stable's second jockey [Pat Walsh] rode Chorelli. I had my horse backed from 7-1 down to 5-2 joint favouritism. The best coups are normally the ones nobody knows about, but the next day my photo was in the papers under the heading 'Big gamble landed.' It might not have been the biggest gamble I was ever involved in, but it was the one that got the most publicity.

McCreevy had never considered racing as a career – 'my mother went to the races all her life and gambled every day, but she had it beaten into us that you had to get on well with your schooling' – and instead became a chartered accountant, before being elected to the Dáil at the age of twenty-seven in 1977. As a finance minister, he was a firm believer that the more tax is cut, the more revenue is raised. One of his earlier moves was to halve capital gains tax to twenty per cent, despite considerable opposition from his civil service advisors, and he succeeded in almost doubling the yield. He also slashed betting tax, and repeatedly lowered income tax.

McCreevy was heavily criticised by opposition politicians for providing financial support to racing ('Charlie's friends in Kildare'), but he has remained an avid racegoer and a close friend of O'Brien. It was McCreevy who first referred to the trainer as 'Ironside'. The politician had in mind, not the field marshal of the Second World War, but the uncompromising wheelchair-bound detective of the television series. The nickname has stuck and is widely used by the jockeys, most of whom belong to a different generation to that of the fictional detective. For them, the iron connotation aptly sums up the tough O'Brien and his hardness towards them.

McCreevy, a Cheltenham regular, was looking forward to Chorelli contesting the 1983 Gold Cup. However, the horse broke a leg in his final race before the Festival, in the PZ Mower Chase at Thurles, and had to be put down. In the next two seasons O'Brien did not have so many good horses, and at the end of 1985 he briefly stopped training. The following year, having leased his stables at Rathbride to trainer Vivian Kennedy, he announced his intention to move to Florida. He had not been feeling well for quite some time and he felt that the warmer climate would improve his health. The stables were sold once Kennedy's twelve-month lease was up, and so was the house in Naas. Ann and daughter Ann-Marie accompanied him to the States, with the intention of buying a place where they could keep young horses and prepare them for racing. 'I felt I should have gone to Florida in the first place, and then we would have made some real money. You

Aidan O'Brien … personal attention right down to the last detail.

The 2001 Shell Champion Hurdle. Istabraq (Charlie Swan) falls at the last, handing the race on a plate to Moscow Flyer and Barry Geraghty.

Before the fall-out with John Magnier. Sir Alex Ferguson is all smiles as he poses with Mick Kinane and Rock Of Gibraltar after the 2002 Irish 2,000 Guineas.

Many apples in the Garden of Eden. Edward O'Grady at the sales searching for the one he wants to pick.

Mucklemeg (Charlie Swan) storms home in the 1994 Cheltenham Bumper to complete a notable double for Edward O'Grady. He also won with Time For A Run that day, his first Festival winners for ten years.

Willie Mullins, delighted at training yet another winner.

Ruby Walsh celebrates as Hedgehunter becomes the first Grand National winner for the Mullins family.

Jim Bolger with son-in-law and stable jockey Kevin Manning.

Teofilo (Kevin Manning) powers home to give Jim Bolger his first National Stakes victory.

Dessie Hughes (trilby) enjoys the presentation following Hardy Eustace's 2003 Cheltenham victory. Tragically Kieran Kelly (right) was killed less than six months later.

Christophe Soumillon is not at his best on Dalakhani in the 2003 Irish Derby. Johnny Murtagh on Alamshar (right) beats him by half a length.

Not much in it at the last in the 2005 Champion Hurdle. Hardy Eustace (Conor O'Dwyer) just leads from Harchibald (Paul Carberry) and Brave Inca (Barry Cash). Macs Joy, who finished fifth, is just behind.

John Oxx … 'training racehorses can be bloody hard work.'

Michael O'Brien, an inspiration to the disabled.

Michael Hourigan's character-filled face.

The 2006 James Nicholson Champion Chase. Beef Or Salmon (Andrew McNamara) is about to lower the colours of Cheltenham Gold Cup winner War Of Attrition (Conor O'Dwyer).

Noel Meade, always cheerful – even in the face of adversity.

The 2005 Champion Hurdle and another Cheltenham near miss for Noel Meade. Halfway up the run-in Paul Carberry sits motionless on Harchibald while Conor O'Dwyer is asking Hardy Eustace for everything.

Vinnie Roe (Pat Smullen) wins the third of his four Irish St Legers, in 2003 at the principal expense of Gamut (Kieren Fallon).

'Inconsistent but on his day a brilliant horse.' Zagreb (Pat Shanahan) springs a 20-1 shock in the 1996 Irish Derby.

David Wachman
listens intently as
Kieren Fallon
reports what
happened.

Jessica Harrington with
Barry Geraghty after
Moscow Flyer's win in
the 2002 Arkle Trophy.

Safely over the last.
Moscow Flyer and
Barry Geraghty win
the 2005 Queen
Mother Champion
Chase from Well Chief
(Timmy Murphy).

can do well out there, training and breaking horses, and in America it doesn't make any difference who you are or what you are. If you are prepared to make the effort, you will make money.'

O'Brien bought a farm and set about turning it into a training stable, but he soon realised he had made a big mistake. Ann missed Ireland, her family and her friends. Her husband's health did improve, but it was of no avail if his wife was going to be unhappy. The more the pair discussed the matter, the more apparent it became that they should return home and try to pick up the pieces. They were back in Ireland within six months of emigrating.

They arrived in County Kildare with no home, stables or horses. Fortunately they found a bungalow they liked, with three acres and twenty boxes, between Naas and Kilcullen. Most of O'Brien's old owners gradually returned to the fold. He modernised the yard, put up more boxes, bought more land and installed an all-weather gallop. His reputation, built in the Bright Highway–King Spruce years, stood him in good stead, but it was not until 1992 that he tasted big race success once more. This was with Vanton in the Irish Grand National, O'Brien's first runner in Irish jumping's richest race since King Spruce, and only his third since he began training. (The first, Eggnog, had finished second in 1980.) Vanton was ridden by twenty-one-year-old Jason Titley, a rising star who had already won that year's Ladbroke, Thyestes Chase and Coral Hurdle Final, and who was to come back from a subsequent barren spell to win the 1995 Grand National on Royal Athlete.

Michael O'Brien has enjoyed considerable success with horses bought out of Flat racing stables. They come on the market in huge quantities each autumn, as trainers weed out their yards to make way for the following season's two-year-olds. These second-hand horses often have as many problems as used cars – they have been galloped, often to the limit, before they are fully mature and the result can be lasting damage. Sifting the wheat from the chaff is a skilled business and

O'Brien himself inspects closely those that come up for sale at Goffs in Ireland, while he usually employs agents to do the same with those offered for sale at Newmarket.

He pays particular attention to the large contingent sold by the Aga Khan at Goffs every year. The Aga's bloodstock tends to be late maturing. John Oxx's patient policy means that they have not been over-tested, and many make good jumpers. O'Brien is seldom outbid when he decides to move for one of these, but in 1992 with Shawiya, a leggy bay considered by some observers to be angular and lacking in scope, he had to go to only 12,000 guineas.

Had she been a colt or gelding, the price would probably have been twice that figure: fillies tend not to do as well as geldings in jump racing. Shawiya proved to be an exception. She won three of her first four starts over hurdles and was a prime contender for the Daily Express Triumph Hurdle, even though no filly had ever won that race. However, O'Brien's plans were thrown into disarray when she was found to have bruising in her near fore hoof three days before the race. He cancelled her place on the plane taking the Irish runners to Cheltenham and rebooked her on the morning of the race. The hoof responded well to treatment, but only after he had schooled her over three flights of hurdles on the morning before the race did O'Brien know she had recovered well enough to make the trip.

At Irish race meetings O'Brien often drives his specially adapted car into the area around the paddock. Sometimes he watches from there, and on other occasions he will go into the parade ring in his wheelchair. But the huge crowds at the Cheltenham Festival make life uncomfortable for wheelchair users, no matter how much the management does to look after their needs. So he stayed at home, reasoning that he would see the race much better on television.

His attention was glued to the screen as Charlie Swan took up a handy position on Shawiya right from the start. She was still travelling well within herself when Swan sent her to the front at the third last flight. She bravely repelled the persistent challenge of Adrian

Maguire's mount Major Bugler, and then the late run of Amazon Express, to go into the history books and credit her trainer with his first success at the most important meeting in jump racing. Shawiya went on to become the first Triumph Hurdle winner to land the Champion Four-Year-Old Hurdle at Punchestown.

The Cheltenham victory was an important one for the disabled. The attendant publicity served as a spur to others similarly afflicted, demonstrating just what can be achieved by those who have lost the use of one or more limbs. O'Brien plays down his own achievement in this regard, pointing out that plenty of other wheelchair-bound people make every bit as much a success of their lives but do not receive the same publicity:

> There are a lot of get-up-and-go people in the Wheelchair Association, but really it all depends on how much you are paralysed. I am paralysed from the chest down which is a bit too high to be really independent, particularly when it comes to stuff like putting the chair in the car, because I have no balance. If I was paralysed only from the waist down, I would be fine.

O'Brien does not like his jockeys going to the front too far out. Those who do so, or who otherwise fail to ride what the trainer regards as a sensible race, can expect a rude reception from the chubby-faced figure with the thinning grey hair when they return to unsaddle. Jason Titley came in after a race at Gowran Park one day to be given such a dressing down, starting with: 'If you ever ride for me again . . .' What made it so much worse for the jockey was that he was ticked off in front of the assembled press corps.

Sometimes O'Brien will criticise jockeys directly to the media. This, understandably, does not go down well either. After Barry Geraghty won the 2005 Pierse Hurdle on Essex, the trainer made no bones about his view that the horse would have won much more easily if the rider had waited longer. Geraghty was even more annoyed when O'Brien's criticism of his handling of Forget The Past at Fairyhouse later the same season also appeared in print. He reasoned that the reporters concerned should have taken the trainer's comments with the grain of salt he believed they deserved, and refrained from repeating them.

O'Brien denies that he is unnecessarily hard on those who ride for him:

> Jockeys are there to ride horses in the proper manner and, if they screw up, they should get told off. If I have a criticism to make, I tell them what they are doing wrong, but I don't go jocking them off. People think I'm tough, and I might come over like that, but I'm not. McCreevy and others gave me that sort of reputation years ago, but on the whole I'm very easy going. As far as I'm concerned, there are only two ways of doing things, the right way and the wrong way. As long as people do things right, there is no problem with me.

Tom Rudd was O'Brien's stable jockey for several years, and gave the trainer his third win in the Irish Grand National when scoring on Glebe Lad in 1999. He provides an interesting assessment of the trainer from a jockey's perspective: 'I had a lot of success for him and he can be a difficult man to ride for, although a fair man. He will never say "well done", but if he doesn't give you a bollocking, it means you've done well!'

Tom Ryan, who joined O'Brien in September 2003 and was the champion claiming rider in 2004/05, provides an equally informative insight from the point of view of a rider still making his way in the racing world:

> Michael is a good man, and his bark is worse than his bite. He can read a race better than anyone I have ever met, and his record as a trainer tells it all. His strike rate is invariably one of the best in the country. He

will tell you where to be at the various stages of a race, and if you stick to that as best you can, you will win nine times out of ten because he almost always has the horses spot on. He will have you spot on as well. He gives you an awful lot of tuition, and that's how you learn.

For much of the 2005/06 season O'Brien's horses were out of sorts after being hit with a low-grade virus which obstinately refused to go away, while Ryan missed much of the campaign through injury. However, he was back in time to win the Pertemps Hurdle at the Cheltenham Festival on Kadoun. The gelding was completely unfancied, despite being owned by J.P. McManus, and started at 50-1.

The bookmakers rarely take such liberties with O'Brien's runners because he has a reputation, well warranted in their eyes, for taking their money. He reckons to have only four or five bets a year, always on his own horses, and he normally shows a profit at the end of each season, 'although not always'. He never backs horses at short prices and often bets in big races, like the Irish National and the Galway Plate, where he can get a good price for his money. But O'Brien has not forgotten the ones that got away early in his training career, and these are where his ambitions lie. 'Soon after I first started, I had two horses capable of winning the Cheltenham Gold Cup, Chorelli and Bright Highway, but neither of them ever got there. I would still love to win that race.'

BIGGEST RACES WON

1980

Mackeson Gold Cup	Bright Highway
Hennessy Gold Cup	Bright Highway

1982
Irish Grand National   King Spruce

1992
Irish Grand National   Vanton

1993
Triumph Hurdle   Shawiya

1999
Irish Grand National   Glebe Lad

2004
Irish Cesarewitch   Essex

2005
Pierse Hurdle   Essex
Totesport Trophy Hurdle   Essex

2006
Pertemps Hurdle   Kadoun

8

MICHAEL HOURIGAN

Most trainers who fail to send out winners in their first season quickly fall by the wayside, and few of those who make the grade can claim such a poor start as Michael Hourigan. After an inauspicious riding career, he held a licence for more than six years before eventually training a winner. Yet he stuck at it through thick and thin, on occasion coming perilously close to financial disaster, and survived to build up one of the most successful jumping yards in Ireland.

Born on 8 December 1947, Hourigan had no family connection with racing except for a nephew of his mother's, Michael Moran, who rode a few winners and became the father of amateur rider Brian Moran. He went into the game because it offered an early escape route from school, and because his small size (he is only 5ft 4in) made him employable. His cattle dealer father and his mother, who ran Hourigan's pub in Rathkeale, decided to send their son to Rockwell College when the teachers at the local national school despaired of ever getting the boy to read and write. At the age of thirteen he had reached fourth class, after being repeatedly held back a year, by the time he went to the famous school just off the Cashel–Cahir main road.

Walter Swinburn became a pupil at Rockwell a dozen years later, and his prowess on the rugby field stayed on in the memory of the masters long after he began to make his mark on the racecourse.

Hardly any of them remembered Hourigan, who left after a year and who by his own admission was not very bright. 'I hated school with a vengeance, but if it hadn't been for Rockwell I might have ended up in Mountjoy Prison. I certainly would not have been able to read or write.'

Michael persuaded his parents that he should go into racing with a view to becoming a jockey. He was only fourteen when he became apprenticed to Dermot Weld's father, Charlie, at Rosewell House on The Curragh in August 1962. An apprentice's life can be tough for a young boy but Hourigan loved it. He enjoyed looking after horses and he liked riding them even more. Riding in races was the biggest thrill of all and, on 50-1 shot Queen's Messenger in the 1965 Irish Cambridgeshire, he came within two and a half lengths of going into the history books. He rode at 6st 7lb, though to look at him today it's hard to imagine. But he never really promised to make the grade and he managed only nine winners during his five-year apprenticeship.

Hourigan then moved to Jimmy O'Connell in the Dublin suburb of Blanchardstown, but the switch was not a success. O'Connell was not prepared to give him the same opportunities as Weld had done, and he was getting heavier. He heard that Wilf Crawford was looking for a lad who could ride in races. Crawford, whose daughter Susan was to become a successful equine artist, trained a small string of jumpers at Haddington in the East Lothian region of Scotland. Hourigan had never so much as schooled a horse over fences, yet he managed to convince Crawford that he was a budding jump jockey. He got the job, and a fortnight later he was given his first taste of National Hunt racing. He was terrified.

It was in a novice chase at Newcastle. It snowed all the way there, and throughout the journey I was praying for the meeting to be called off. There were twenty-three runners and I had never seen so many fallers. They went down like ninepins. Only three of them survived.

Fortunately, my horse was one of them and I finished second. I never really had the nerve for race-riding and eventually it gave me up.

He was soon back at Rosewell House, but it was an on-off relationship. He left a few weeks after his return; a fortnight later, Weld's wife Gita rang him to say they were short of staff and would he come back? He did, but again not for long. He continued his employment on much the same intermittent basis until August the following year, when a chance meeting at the Tralee racing festival led to him being offered a job with Lord Petersham and his small string of jumpers at Patrickswell, not far from Rathkeale. Hourigan rode two of his four jumping winners for Petersham before the pair parted company in unhappy circumstances (Hourigan was fired) in 1970.

Hourigan helped out in his mother's pub, and the two stables at the back of it inspired him to start training. Hugh McMahon, a business-man who owned a sizeable part of the old Limerick racecourse and who had bought the land where the new one was built, trained a few horses of his own under permit. Hourigan sold him a horse called Born To Win, whom he had bought from Francis Flood for £200. McMahon was charged £250, but he said that his previous owner could get him ready for the racecourse. The gelding was still with Hourigan when he lived up to his name in a bumper at Mallow (now Cork racecourse) in May 1972. However, Hourigan received no credit for the success because McMahon was the official trainer.

Certain that he had what it took to make it as a trainer, Hourigan applied for a licence the following year and at Killarney in May 1975 he was first past the post in a hunter chase with Mon Capriole. There should have been a big celebration in the pub that evening but the stewards had other ideas, taking the race off Mon Capriole for causing interference and relegating him to second place. The trainer is convinced that he should have got off the mark in a maiden hurdle at Tralee the following year, but the horse's rider mistook the winning post and was beaten in a photo finish.

Hourigan was still operating from the stables behind the pub, which he renamed the Horse and Jockey. To make ends meet, he ran a horse transport business; at least he drove his own lorry to the sales and wherever else he thought he could pick up a customer. Many a time he wanted to give up training, but he persevered, not least because he felt he knew little else outside racing and the pub.

That long-awaited first winner came on St Patrick's Day 1979, when Jackie Cullen (uncle of jump jockey John Cullen) rode 14-1 chance Ramrajya to a narrow win in a handicap hurdle at Limerick. Hourigan's name finally entered the record books, even though the official form book spelt it Hourican. (The majority of racegoers to this day pronounce his name incorrectly as 'Hore-rigan', although the trainer calls himself 'How-rigan'. He also refers to himself as Mike, whereas he is almost universally addressed as Michael and occasionally as Mick.) But Ramrajya's win was infinitely more important than getting his name right: 'Throughout those six years, I felt that even training one winner would satisfy my ambitions. I was struggling all the time, and learning through my mistakes. I often ran horses just for the sake of having a runner, and sometimes I would jar them up as a result.'

Ramrajya really started the ball rolling. He won two of his next three races, and finished 1979 with five winners to his credit. The following year he had twelve, and the short, stocky figure (it had broadened considerably since his riding days) with the ruddy complexion and character-filled face began to become familiar to the regulars on Irish racecourses. Those unaware of his background sometimes looked at the flattened nose and wondered if he had been a boxer's sparring partner who had received too many punches.

The trainer's problems switched from attempting to train a winner to trying to find stables and gallops for his rapidly growing string. Many of his horses were housed in various backyard stables within striking distance of the pub, and were worked wherever their trainer found an open gate and an uncomplaining farmer. He rented an old stud with stables and a cottage, but the pub and its customers were still an important source of income. They also took up time that would have been better spent in well-earned sleep: 'I would often return home from an evening meeting at 11 p.m., and there would be people in the bar. I would have a jar with them, and it could be 4 a.m. before I went to bed. I had to get up at six to go to the yard.'

In 1985 he bought sixty-seven acres on the Limerick side of Adare for £110,000, paying a ten per cent deposit, and the vendor obligingly said he could move his horses there straight away. However, Hourigan had no idea how he would raise the balance of the purchase price. As he searched for ways of doing so – and failed to find any – he seriously considered pulling out of the deal and forfeiting his deposit. Only two things stopped him: the fact that his horses were already there, and the support of his bank manager, Jerry O'Connell.

Hourigan and his wife Anne – they had married three months after Ramrajya's first win – plus their growing family, moved into the property's dilapidated two-up and two-down cottage, which had not been lived in for fourteen years. They built the first block of stables on to the side of the cottage and started on the gallops, repeatedly going to the bank for assistance.

Things didn't come easily for us. We were in trouble with the bank more often than not, and if I'd had another bank manager I might not have got there. Jerry believed in me, and his back was to the wall several times because of me. Thank God Tattersalls and Goffs gave credit. You could always tell them that the cheque was in the post, and I would often not sign it in order to get another fortnight. Even so, I would never have survived had I not sold the good horses, and got my percentage of the sales proceeds.

The good ones that Hourigan sold included Kilbrittain Castle, Very Promising, Stray Shot and Deep Bramble, although the last-named left only after giving him his first big wins in the 1993 Kerry National and Ericsson Chase. From that point on, Hourigan was sufficiently strong financially to be able to hold on to many of his best horses – although he continued to sell some of them, notably Amberleigh House, who went on to win the 2004 Grand National.

Hourigan has continually expanded his stabling, his landholding and the facilities of his training establishment. He now owns 250 acres and in 1995, with the last of his five children on the way, he finally set about building a house. Part-way through the construction, he learnt that an adjoining twenty acres was about to come on the market. Building was immediately suspended, and his wife reluctantly agreed to continue living in the cottage adjoining the stables while money was raised for the land.

Today Hourigan is worth several million euro, yet his policy with horses is still to buy at the bottom end of the market. Horses at bloodstock auctions are carefully graded by the sales companies so that buyers do not have to waste time attending every sale, or even every day of any sale that caters for their shopping list. Hourigan is one of the few who attends every sale in Ireland, and he is there from first lot in the morning almost until the hammer falls for the final time in the evening.

I like buying and selling – don't forget, my father was a cattle dealer – and I buy cheaply because I have had to suit my pocket. I buy horses for myself, rarely for clients, and even when I have a client in mind, he doesn't have to take the horse if he decides he doesn't want the animal. For a long time I had a thing that five grand was my limit. It's very easy to buy the best horse in the sale – everybody knows which that one is – and I often buy somebody else's leavings. It's what takes your fancy. It's a bit like going to a dance. Just as you see some fine, good-looking women so I'm looking for something that catches the eye, something that can walk and that I can improve. If the engine is there, I will find it. I've had more success with the cheap ones. I go to the sales to buy

racehorses, and if it was just money that bought racehorses, I would
never have got where I am today.

Hourigan has long maintained that the horse who made him was not
Deep Bramble but Dorans Pride, who won thirty races including the
1995 Stayers' Hurdle: 'when the Cheltenham commentator called out
"look at Dorans Pride on the outside, he's running away", my head
went cold and I couldn't wait for him to jump the last.' This tough
gelding recovered from a near-fatal attack of colic in the season after
his Festival win to become a high-class chaser, and he twice finished
third in the Cheltenham Gold Cup. But eyebrows were raised when
Hourigan brought him out of retirement to run him in point-to-
points and hunter chases at the age of fourteen. Tragedy struck in the
Foxhunters at Cheltenham where Dorans Pride fell at the second
fence, breaking a leg and having to be put down. The fatal fall was a
body blow for Hourigan, coming only three-quarters of an hour after
Beef Or Salmon's early exit in the Cheltenham Gold Cup. He was
widely criticised for subjecting such an old horse, particularly one
who had served him so well, to the rigours of the Festival, and he
received several vitriolic letters. He defends himself, claiming that the
horse died doing what he loved most:

Losing him was a shock to me. I never thought he would break a leg
but I felt sorry for my family more than for myself, particularly for my
daughter Kay who loved him. People say that he should have gone into
retirement and stayed there, but I knew him better than anybody and
he would never have been happy in retirement. He was put down
doing what he loved, and he could not have chosen a better scene than
the Cheltenham Festival.

Tropical Lake gave the trainer his first winner in Britain when she
won the Glenlivet Anniversary Hurdle at the 1994 Grand National

meeting, and he experienced just as much satisfaction when the horse landed the following year's Irish Lincoln. Hourigan loves having a crack at a big Flat race with his jumpers: Dorans Pride was to win the Leopardstown November Handicap in 2000. Deejaydee had given him a second Cheltenham winner in the previous year's National Hunt Chase, but success in either of the two big races at Galway eluded him until Rockholm Boy triumphed in the 2002 Plate.

My father, who died before I trained a winner, used to go to Galway and I remember him talking about the Plate, although in those days I never thought I would have a horse to win the race. Before Rockholm Boy, I thought my best chance was with a mare called Regent's Pride, but she was taken away from me and sent to Paddy Mullins. Joe Byrne rode her in the 1985 race, but she had to tell you when she was ready to go, and she was quite capable of pulling herself up if you went too soon with her. Joe kicked for touch at the top of the hill, and she looked a certainty. I knew her bolt would be shot when she met the rising ground, and she finished fifth. I think I would have won with her. Rockholm Boy was owned by a Galway man, and I laid the horse out for the Plate a year in advance. I never knew that there was such a spin-off to winning the race. It brought me new owners and quite a few horses. We don't get the same television publicity in Ireland that they do in England, and televised races here are hard won.

There was no shortage of publicity with Beef Or Salmon, a horse who owed his unusual name to the limited fare on offer at a hotel where Hourigan once stopped for a meal. (He was informed that everything on the menu was off bar beef or salmon.) The horse had no name, and little to recommend him, when the trainer bought him as a four-year-old for £6,500 at Goffs in June 2000. There was almost nothing of note in the pedigree, and his tail was so short and awkward-looking that some observers thought it had been broken.

However, Hourigan saw something in the horse – he can't pinpoint quite what – and it was not long before the gelding began to show him that his judgement was spot on. Prospective buyers were less impressed and two deals fell through before Ballymena hotelier Dan McLarnon and his friend Joe Craig, a retired businessman from Castledawson, made the long journey from Northern Ireland to County Limerick towards the end of 2000 to see their horse Annaghmore Gale.

Beef Or Salmon was pointed out to them and they were told that, if they wanted to buy another horse, this was the one to get because he was going to be good. The pair ended up paying Hourigan £15,000, and there were two contingency payments – £5,000 if the gelding won a point-to-point and another £10,000 if he won a bumper. McLarnon and Craig travelled back to the North with Seamus McCloy, who had two useful horses with Hourigan, Hi Cloy and Tell The Nipper. Told halfway home that he could have a third share for £50,000 sterling, McCloy burst out laughing. But the joke was on him when the owners were offered £400,000 after Beef Or Salmon's second bumper win.

The gelding failed to live up to his bumper promise over hurdles, but it was quite a different story when Hourigan put him over fences. The traditional starting point is a beginners' or novice chase, but Hourigan thought so much of the horse that he started him off against seasoned campaigners in a Grade Two chase. It was almost unheard of for a trainer to pitch a horse in at the deep end on his first race over fences, yet Beef Or Salmon won the Morris Oil Chase at Clonmel with ease, jumping every fence like an experienced handicapper. He followed up in almost as good a race at Cork before winning two top-class chases at Leopardstown, each time producing a devastating turn of foot when the tap was turned on. He started second favourite for the Cheltenham Gold Cup – and precious few novices have ever done enough to warrant that sort of support – but took a crashing fall at the third fence.

Beef Or Salmon won only two of his first four starts the following season, and when he came in after finishing a poor third in the

Ericsson Chase at the Leopardstown Christmas meeting, jockey Timmy Murphy told Hourigan that there was something radically wrong. Bill Murphy, the trainer's regular vet, called in equine physiotherapist Liz Kent. She informed Hourigan that the horse would be unable to run for five months and that, if it was David Beckham or Roy Keane who was suffering this type of injury, they would be having physiotherapy for eight hours a day. Beef Or Salmon had muscle problems in his back, neck, shoulder and groin, which could be traced back to the Cheltenham fall; whenever the horse was asked to exert himself, he saved himself on the affected areas by putting the strain on other parts of his body.

Kent and Hourigan's daughter Kay, the stable's head groom, put in a huge amount of work in order to sort out the horse's problems in time for the Cheltenham Gold Cup, and Murphy gave him a peach of a patient ride to finish fourth. However, he disappointed in the 2005 race, and did so again in each of the next two years. The fast pace and the good going on which the Gold Cup is normally run did not seem to suit Beef Or Salmon who, like many of Ireland's Cheltenham disappointments, is at his best in testing conditions where the pace is, of necessity, much slower.

However, all the publicity generated by the horse raised Hourigan's profile, bringing more new owners than even Rockholm Boy had done. Beef Or Salmon certainly brought more phone calls from the press: 'The media interest can be annoying sometimes, and it gets a bit much as Cheltenham nears, but publicity in the papers, no matter whether it's good or bad, is still publicity. We need the papers as much as they need us, and I can handle it.'

Hourigan can also handle the strain attached to training such a big-name horse. He insists that he is not one of those who goes down to the yard every morning saying his prayers that the stable star is all right. 'If he isn't, what can I do about it?' Hourigan reasons, pointing out that a trainer has to live with the risk of something going wrong. 'If you don't drive your car every day, then you won't get a puncture.

But I have very good gallops and I don't do anything stupid. If I ever have any doubts about doing anything, then I don't do it.'

For a man whose success in the saddle was so limited, Hourigan has been remarkably good at turning out jockeys. Those whom he has groomed for stardom include Adrian Maguire, Timmy Murphy, Shane Broderick, Robbie Supple, Johnny Kavanagh and his two elder sons Michael and Paul. The former was champion amateur in Britain in the 1991/92 season, and Paul promised to be even better until weight problems forced him on to the sidelines. Laura, the trainer's younger daughter, is another very good rider.

Maguire stresses that Hourigan gives everyone who works for him a chance to prove how good they can be. For his part, the trainer firmly believes that his own lack of success in the saddle has had a big bearing on his ability to bring out the best in others:

> In my day you either had it, or you hadn't. There was nobody to bring it out of you. I'm not complaining, that's just the way it was. I knew what to do but I couldn't do it, so I wasn't very good. But if I see that somebody has potential, I want to teach them, and I want to teach them properly. When you have a good kid, it's a pleasure to work with him but I will be hard on him and he has to be able to take it. If he has the patience to stay with me, work and listen to what I say, then I will help him all the way.

Maguire had ridden 250 winners on the pony racing circuit before he joined Hourigan, but the trainer found this achievement more of a drawback than an advantage. 'You couldn't tell him anything – he knew too much – and it took me a long time to train him. If I gave him a bollocking, he would not even look at me for the next twenty-four hours.'

Surprisingly, Hourigan did not consider Maguire a natural, and to begin with the teenager showed his boss nothing to suggest that he was going to become a top jockey. But Maguire made the most of the opportunities Hourigan gave him in point-to-points and one day at Dromahane in County Cork he rode six winners. What impressed Hourigan was that few of the six horses had shown much promise, and nor did they do so subsequently.

Maguire became champion point-to-point rider of Ireland, and he was still only nineteen when he won the 1991 Irish National on Omerta. He was promptly head-hunted by Toby Balding and won the following season's Cheltenham Gold Cup on Cool Ground. He spent the rest of a brilliant career in Britain and, while he was never champion jockey, he rode 194 winners in the 1993/94 season and lost out on the title to Richard Dunwoody by only three. A broken neck in a fall at Warwick in 2002 ended his riding days, and he now trains at Lombardstown in County Cork.

Shane Broderick also broke a bone in his neck, but he was not so lucky. He was only twenty-two and had already ridden a Cheltenham winner on Dorans Pride when a harmless-looking fall on the unfortunately named Another Deadly, in a chase at Fairyhouse on the day of the 1997 Irish National, condemned him to a wheelchair for the rest of his life. It was the sort of fall that jump jockeys walk away from unscathed every day of their working lives, but Broderick hit the ground head first and the impact broke the spinal cord at the base of his neck. Other jump jockeys had been paralysed in the past, notably Paddy Farrell, Tim Brookshaw and Michael O'Brien, but none of these severed their spine so high up. As a result, none was paralysed to the same extent as the luckless Broderick, who has little or no movement below the neck. He had been tutored by Hourigan, and had progressed to stable jockey long before that fateful fall. The trainer had become close to him; he and Anne were frequent visitors during the year Broderick spent in hospital, and have been so ever since at the house specially built for him between Birr and Portumna in County Offaly. Indeed, Hourigan was instrumental in Broderick's decision to take out a licence to train horses.

Timmy Murphy also had problems, albeit of a very different

nature. He was still an amateur when he left Hourigan and, although widely regarded as having outstanding talent, he lost his first job in Britain – as conditional rider to Kim Bailey – for bad time-keeping. He bounced back to become first jockey for Paul Nicholls, but some owners preferred the up-and-coming Joe Tizzard. Murphy's position later became more secure but he had serious problems with alcohol. In 2001 he was banned from driving for four years, and he also received a community service order for 110 hours.

However, these offences were nothing compared to what happened in April 2002, when Murphy returned from Tokyo after riding the Nicholls-trained Cenkos in the Nakayama Grand Jump. He was seen drinking vodka and orange (Murphy later claimed it was just orange juice) before the flight and, travelling first class, he spent two hours at the plane's bar drinking wine. He assaulted a female flight attendant and urinated against the flight deck door before sleeping for the rest of the journey, and he could remember neither incident when he was arrested at Heathrow. Murphy was sentenced to six months in prison for indecent assault and being drunk on an aircraft.

He was released early for good behaviour, and a fortnight before he came out of prison Hourigan received a phone call from Murphy's agent, Chris Broad. Murphy wanted to return to his old mentor for a week. He arrived at the yard within forty-eight hours of his release, and spent the time riding as many horses as he could.

We had not parted on the best of terms when he left here the first time. I thought that he was lazy and that he had a chip on his shoulder, but we were delighted to have him back. Drink can do things to you, and he was a man who was down. He was very light, and he had lost a lot of weight after his time in prison. We didn't speak much about his experience, and all he wanted to do was to get focused on what he is good at. The first day he rode out seven or eight horses and he was bolloxed, but after a week he was back race-riding. He is now a better jockey than before he went to prison, and a better man.

Murphy had a tendency to be unduly hard on his mounts, which was a major factor in some of Nicholls's owners preferring Tizzard, but prison changed his whole approach. He became an exceptionally patient and supremely stylish rider, frequently dropping his mounts out in the course of a race and bringing them with a superbly timed late run, and he was sparing in his use of the whip. He struck up a most successful partnership with Beef Or Salmon and several other Hourigan horses. He also adopted the Alcoholics Anonymous creed of living for the day and refusing to look to the future.

Michael Hourigan has a great sense of humour and often roars with laughter at the quips he makes. 'We've gone upmarket, we've now got a secretary,' he told the press on their visit to the yard shortly before Cheltenham in 2003. 'But I'm still sleeping with the old one.' He also delights in pretending to speak bluntly to those he knows well. Racing journalists, ringing him on his mobile, are often greeted with 'What the fuck's wrong with you now?'

He can speak bluntly to his staff, and mean it. 'If a horse gets hurt in the yard through stupidity, I can explode.' At one time he would attempt to bring off gambles, but repeated losses taught him to look elsewhere for income.

I was a bad failure at betting. Now I just look at the racecard, calculate my percentage and say to myself that this is a little bit extra for a job I am paid to do and which I love . . .

What I particularly enjoy is nurturing horses from being babies to winning races, and the real satisfaction comes from winning with a bad one. Anybody can win with a good horse, and I get a real kick out of winning with one that's not much good. I wouldn't say that it's better than winning at Cheltenham which is the Olympics of jump racing, but I regard it as a feather in my cap.

But that first winner of all has never been forgotten, and the photograph of Ramrajya in his house serves a special purpose:

> If things are bad, and I haven't trained a winner for a while, I'll look at
> that picture and think 'things can't be that fucking bad'. It took me six
> years to get that far, and I would have been happy just to train a few
> winners and be struggling. In those early days my wife and I never even
> dreamed we would be where we are today.

BIGGEST RACES WON

1993

Kerry National	Deep Bramble
Ericsson Chase	Deep Bramble

1994

Glenlivet Anniversary Hurdle	Tropical Lake

1995

Ladbroke Hurdle	Anusha
Irish Lincolnshire	Tropical Lake
Hatton's Grace Hurdle	Dorans Pride
Stayers' Hurdle	Dorans Pride

1997

Kerry National	Dorans Pride

1998

Leopardstown Hennessy Gold Cup	Dorans Pride
Ericsson Chase	Dorans Pride

1999
National Hunt Chase   Deejaydee
Paddy Power Handicap Chase   Inis Cara

2000
Leopardstown November Handicap   Dorans Pride

2002
Galway Plate   Rockholm Boy
Ericsson Chase   Beef Or Salmon

2003
Leopardstown Hennessy Gold Cup   Beef Or Salmon
Kerry National   Native Performance

2004
Punchestown Gold Cup   Beef Or Salmon
James Nicholson Champion Chase   Beef Or Salmon
Lexus Chase   Beef Or Salmon

2005
Lexus Chase   Beef Or Salmon

2006
Leopardstown Hennessy Gold Cup   Beef Or Salmon
James Nicholson Champion Chase   Beef Or Salmon

2007
Leopardstown Hennessy Gold Cup   Beef Or Salmon

9

NOEL MEADE

Cheltenham, 14 March 2000. Sausalito Bay has just come home in front in the Supreme Novices' Hurdle. The tall figure in the trilby, beaming from ear to ear, kneels down in the winner's enclosure and kisses the grass. Many of the large crowd burst out laughing. Others cheer. They know what this moment means to the Irish trainer, and they have some idea of the trials and tribulations he has suffered in his quest to win at the biggest meeting in the National Hunt calendar.

Noel Meade had ambitions of becoming a jockey but it is as a trainer that he has made his name, and in recent seasons he has dominated the National Hunt lists. His stable is one of the most powerful in jump racing, yet for much of his career he was haunted by a Cheltenham hoodoo. Success at the Festival constantly eluded him and year after year he would return to Ireland cursing his luck. Little wonder that when he finally trained a winner at the meeting, nearly thirty years after he first took out a licence, he made that now famous gesture.

Many Irish farmers keep a broodmare or two on their land, and it is not so long ago that almost all of them did. But there were none on the 400-acre farm at Castletown Kilpatrick, on the road between Navan in County Meath and Kingscourt in County Cavan, when Noel Meade and his brother Ben were growing up. Their father had no interest in racing or horses, and for most of his life he maintained that they were a sure way of going broke. He had his children late in life, and he looked on in quiet amusement as the boys rode their ponies and became avid supporters of the Meath football team. His elder son has hardly missed a county championship match ever since, but while Noel soon realised that lack of ability meant that he would never be able to don the famous green and gold jersey, he was convinced that racing could be a different story.

Born on 2 January 1951, Meade dreamed of becoming a jockey even before he started racing his pony at the local gymkhanas when he was twelve. These races were taken seriously by the participants, although they were nothing like as well organised as the pony races on which the likes of Charlie Swan, Tommy Carmody and others were reared. The tall, thin Meade passed the post in front more than a dozen times in these gymkhana races and, when he was fifteen, he began to ride in a few of the 'proper' pony races.

Three years later he progressed to the racecourse. He and a friend clubbed together to buy a gelding called Tu Va for £100. Meade applied to the Turf Club for a permit to train the horse, and for another to enable him to ride it in races. Eventually, in an amateur riders' maiden hurdle at Wexford in August 1971, Meade rode into the winner's enclosure. The twenty-year-old touched his cap in acknowledgement of the applause, convinced this was just the start of a career packed with winners, but he never rode another.

He has vivid memories of one that got away at Galway. 'It was in an amateur handicap hurdle, and again I rode Tu Va. I jumped the last hurdle in the lead, and then looked round. Tu Va would stop as soon as he hit the front and, by the time I looked back, Mouse Morris had swept past and beaten me. Dermot Weld was third in that race, and John Burke fourth.'

Meade's father was an old man by now and he decided to hand over the farm to his two sons. Ben became a farmer, like his father, while his elder brother resolved to turn his half into a training establishment. Ben found it hard to make a decent living after the turn of the millennium, despite the huge financial benefits the European Union brought to Irish farming, and following discussions between the two brothers it was decided that he would instead assist Noel with the running of the training business.

As for Noel himself, that Wexford success, and the exposure gained from riding in races, attracted offers from owners, and in 1972 he went back to the Turf Club to trade in his permit for a full licence. He began with four horses and by the end of the year he had trained four more winners. Owners began to take note of the 6ft 1in youngster with the loping stride and infectious enthusiasm for life. In 1973 he had a string of eight, the following year it was sixteen and by 1975 his stable had increased to thirty. However, the training fees were low and finances were tight. Rather than build a block of stables, Meade added a new box each time he was sent an extra horse. He spent the mornings doing the training, and the afternoons working as a blocklayer and roofer.

As the building work increased, so his race riding diminished, and soon he stopped altogether. 'I was never good enough, and people kept telling me I should give it up.' But the part played by Tu Va in his life has never been forgotten: Meade named his house and stables after the horse.

The old saying that success breeds success is particularly applicable in racing, where newspaper publicity acts as a free advertisement for the skills of those who send out winners. In addition, many owners want a trainer who can enjoy success with them – and for these Meade was their man. Young and keen, he was full of optimism and capable of celebrating late into the night. His ever-present cheerfulness, even in the face of adversity, was another major plus. 'I could never see the point of going around with a long face,' he reasons. 'I am a firm believer that there is only one way to look at things, and that is on the bright side.'

It's an admirable philosophy, but one which few of us are able to adopt, no matter how much we might like to. Some of those who know Meade well have on occasion queried how he manages it. After Meath had been beaten in a Leinster final a few years ago, one of the supporters leaving the ground alongside Meade remarked that he was taking the disappointment remarkably well. 'I've got used to it,' came the reply. 'I have to. I get beaten on the racetrack every day of the week.' With that, he burst out laughing. The humour was so infectious that the dejected supporter also roared with laughter.

Even today, after more than three decades of the ups and downs of training horses, Meade's almost boyish enthusiasm is as strong as ever. In the winner's enclosure, after witnessing a particularly promising performance from one of his potential stars, he will rock from one leg to the other in excitement as he talks about what is clearly one of the apples of his eye.

One of the best at Tu Va in the early years was a filly called Sweet Mint. She won as a two-year-old in 1976 and four times the following season. After she had run a big race to take third in the Greenlands Stakes at The Curragh on the day of the Irish 2,000 Guineas, Meade decided to send her to Royal Ascot for the Cork & Orrery Stakes. This quality sprint was flying high, and the filly was ignored in the betting at 20-1. But Wally Swinburn sent her to the front well over a furlong out, and she kept up the gallop to beat the following season's King's Stand and Prix de l'Abbaye winner Double Form by half a length. Noel Meade was well and truly on the map, and he began 1979 with more than sixty horses. One of them, La Samanna, finished second in the Irish 1,000 Guineas.

Unusually for one who was having such success, Meade was entirely self-taught. He had never spent time learning the ropes with an experienced trainer, and in his early years he sometimes wondered if he should have done. In moments of self-doubt, he comforted himself with the thought that, had he done so, he would have learnt only that particular trainer's way of doing things. Better, or so he told himself, to learn as he was going along.

The vast majority of his horses were dual purpose: they ran on the Flat as well as over jumps, and they tended to run a lot. Batista ran fourteen times in 1979, winning once on the Flat and twice over hurdles. The second of the jump wins came in the Sean Graham Juvenile Champion Hurdle at Leopardstown on St Stephen's Day, a sure sign that the horse was a prime contender for the Triumph Hurdle. However, he was only fourth in the Victor Ludorum Hurdle at Haydock twelve days before the Triumph, and as a result he started among the 50-1 shots at Cheltenham.

In those days Meade put up Joe Byrne on most of his jumpers. Byrne, Irish champion in 1979, rode with more determination than polish and placed considerable reliance on the whip. It was his practice, when riding a finish, to swing his arm so that he hit his mounts down the shoulder and then behind the saddle in the same movement. He did not normally hit them particularly hard, but his style lacked finesse and would have seen him repeatedly suspended today.

Byrne sent Batista to the front at the second last, but he was headed by Tommy Carmody on Starfen approaching the final flight and hampered in the process. Starfen then fell, leaving Batista in front. Meade was watching the race, in a state of high excitement, on the lawn halfway between the last hurdle and the winning post.

When Starfen fell, Heighlin was beginning to challenge but he was hampered and he stopped almost to a walk. Joe promptly went for his stick on Batista. If he had held the horse together and straightened him up, we would probably have won. When he and Heighlin flashed past the post together, I thought we were beaten. Then somebody told me my horse had won. I ran like hell to the winner's enclosure. At least, I did until I got close enough to see the expression on Joe's face!

It was the first of a series of misfortunes at Cheltenham that were to dog Meade for the next twenty years, but at the time all the talk was about the treatment handed out to Byrne and Edward O'Grady's jockey, Tommy Ryan. The latter was fined for excessive use of the whip after winning the Stayers' Hurdle on Mountrivers on the opening day of the meeting. Less than twenty-four hours later, he was in far more serious trouble. He rode Drumlargan in the SunAlliance Novices' Hurdle, but the hot favourite tried to duck out towards the chute that leads from the paddock after jumping the final flight. In order to straighten him up, Ryan hit his mount several times across the face and on his neck. He made more conventional use of the whip in the closing stages, but he applied it vigorously, and at least once after passing the post.

The stewards referred his riding to the Jockey Club's Disciplinary Committee. They also 'sent on' Byrne for excessive use of the whip on Batista, not least because he had been fined for a similar offence on another horse earlier the same month. Both jockeys were suspended from riding for three months. It was a harsh penalty, although supported by many members of the British media. Brough Scott wrote in the *Sunday Times* that the pair's 'heavy-handed methods offended anyone who hates seeing a racehorse treated like some wretched Spanish donkey late for market'. The press in Ireland were equally critical of the Jockey Club for over-reacting.

However, in the short term at least, Batista's defeat proved only a temporary setback for his trainer, who was still only twenty-nine. He continued to turn out the winners, and he finished the year as the leading trainer in Ireland in terms of races won, with sixty-seven winners. He soon became one of the principal trainers to follow at festival meetings, particularly at Galway. In 1981 he sent out Pinch Hitter to win the McDonogh Handicap, and the following evening he won the John Player Amateur Handicap with Steel Duke, who went on to land the Bass Gold Cup at Tralee, the seventh of the horse's eight wins that year.

The 1982 success story was Pinch Hitter, who won five of his seven starts including the valuable Hennessy Handicap at Leopardstown, the McDonogh and the Galway Hurdle. 'That Galway win was the best day of my life,' Meade recalled many years later, adding with considerable overstatement, 'We celebrated for a year.'

Pinch Hitter also won the following year's Galway Hurdle, and on both occasions he was ridden by Jonjo O'Neill. Pinch Hitter was not the only horse to win the same big race in those two years, for Five Nations landed back-to-back runnings of the Irish Cesarewitch. He was ridden by Willie Carson and trained by Gillian O'Brien for her father, Phonsie.

Phonsie, christened Alphonsus, was a younger brother of Vincent O'Brien. He had been a brave and talented amateur rider who finished second on Royal Tan in the 1951 Grand National, and might well have won had his mount not made a terrible mistake at the final fence. He later turned to training, and in the 1960s he won four consecutive runnings of the Galway Plate.

Meade had married Carmel Geraghty when he was only twenty-three. His bride had thrown herself into her husband's chosen way of life with enthusiasm, and had also taken on the role of assistant trainer. However, relations between the pair deteriorated and they decided to split up. Meade was taken with Gillian O'Brien, and the more they saw of each other, the closer they became. Gillian decided to give up her own training ambitions to move in with Noel and help him in the business. She has been an invaluable asset.

Meade acquired horses like Steel Duke and Pinch Hitter through his policy of buying big yearling colts with staying pedigrees. His theory was that, if they failed to make the grade on the Flat, they would have every chance of being successful over jumps. However, economics periodically persuaded him to go for a better type of yearling and put the emphasis more on Flat racing: 'There was not a lot of money in jump racing, and the only time you could really make money out of a jumper was when you sold him. Naturally, when you have a good one you don't want to sell, but you almost had to.'

On the Flat, Rangoon Ruby won the 1985 Phoenix Sprint Stakes, and two years later Taking Steps finished third in the Irish 1,000 Guineas, while the following season Little Bighorn was fourth in the Irish Derby. However, Meade refused to give up training jumpers, and to this day he is convinced that he should have won the 1986 Galway Hurdle with Fane Ranger. No English-trained horse had ever won the race until Ray Peacock decided to send Rushmoor from his stables near Tarporley in Cheshire. Rushmoor, bred by the Queen, had some useful form but was given only 10st 6lb in the big Galway prize. Peter Scudamore made all the running on the gelding to beat Fane Ranger by eight lengths, much to Meade's disgust.

> Fane Ranger had top weight of twelve stone, and the handicapper underestimated Rushmoor's weight. I can remember working out before the race that, if I had put Fane Ranger in the Scottish Champion Hurdle [a handicap at that time], and the handicapper used Rushmoor's Irish mark as a line, then my horse would have been giving the triple Champion Hurdle winner See You Then three pounds!

Meade had several Cheltenham runners in the decade after Batista, although none came anywhere near as close to winning, but in 1992 he was convinced that he had a near-certainty for the Champion Bumper. Tiananmen Square failed to find a buyer when offered for sale as a yearling, and was 'bought-in' by a syndicate of pinhookers (people who buy horses as foals intending to sell them on as yearlings). They sent him to Meade with a view to finding a buyer the following season, but the horse was so backward that, not only did nobody want him, he could not be trained. It was the same when the horse was a three-year-old, and Meade decided to put him away for a bumper.

John Magnier bought the horse before he made his debut at Naas early in 1992. Tiananmen Square was not quite four, yet he won in impressive style by five lengths. At Fairyhouse five weeks later he won by a distance, but it was what happened at home that convinced Meade that at last he had a Cheltenham winner. Three weeks before the Festival, he worked Tiananmen Square with a decent miler, and watched in growing excitement as his Champion Bumper hope galloped all over his rival. 'I was convinced that Tiananmen Square was rather more than the best bumper horse I had ever had. I felt he was capable of winning almost any Flat race I might care to put him into.'

Meade had overlooked a horse called Montelado, and the bad luck that Batista had presaged twelve years earlier. Tiananmen Square pulled ten lengths clear of all the others as he galloped up the final hill at Cheltenham, but he was still a dozen lengths behind Montelado at the line.

That evening Gillian drove her dispirited partner up the motorway to Birmingham airport, with Meade running the race over in his mind time and time again. He still could not believe that Tiananmen Square had been beaten so comprehensively. Gillian, to comfort him as much as anything else, pointed out that their horse would have run out a wide-margin winner had Montelado not been in the field. 'You're right,' exclaimed Meade, and as if to reinforce the point he slammed his hand against the windscreen of the hire car. The glass smashed into tiny fragments and, once he had pushed his fist through to let Gillian see where she was going, he burst out laughing.

His conviction that he had the better horse was borne out at Punchestown seven weeks later when Tiananmen Square reversed the placings with his Cheltenham conqueror, although the altered weights suggested that he would only just have beaten Montelado even if he had run up to his best in the Champion Bumper.

The following year Meade had a horse who, although not as good as Tiananmen Square, had the ability to make amends in the same race. Unfortunately, Heist was beaten by half a length. His trainer put the defeat down to pilot error:

Charlie Swan rode Heist in a piece of work at Fairyhouse with some very good horses, and my fellow absolutely annihilated them, and as a result Charlie was very confident of winning. In fact, I think he was over-confident. He was a bit far out of his ground coming down the hill and, as we found out later in the horse's career, stamina was Heist's forte. Turning into the straight, he was so far back that he had no chance, yet he flew home and he was only just beaten.

Swan also got the blame in 1996, although not from Meade. In the Triumph Hurdle, the Irish champion rode Magical Lady for Aidan O'Brien while Meade's Embellished was ridden by Paul Carberry. As the runners headed towards the final flight, Magical Lady and Mistinguett, ridden by Carl Llewellyn, were fighting it out. But Carberry was sitting only just behind them, and seemingly going much the best of the three. Then Magical Lady veered to the left, hampering Embellished so badly that Carberry's mount lost his footing and fell. The stewards ruled that Swan was guilty of irresponsible riding. They suspended him for six days and disqualified Magical Lady from second place.

Swan was convinced he was hard done by and that the fault lay with Llewellyn, who had crossed over on to the chase course in a bid to save ground and had then tried to come up Swan's inside, a cardinal sin in the eyes of jockeys. As Mistinguett rejoined the hurdles course, Embellished swerved away from him and caught the heels of Magical Lady. This was not clear on the patrol film, which suggested that the blame lay with Swan, but the aerial view on the Channel 4 rerun showed quite clearly that the fault lay with Llewellyn. He admitted this when Swan met up with him at Punchestown the following month. It was little consolation to Swan, and even less to Meade, who was by now convinced that Cheltenham had a jinx on him.

Two years later his bad luck struck again. In the Arkle Trophy, Hill Society and the Martin Pipe-trained Champleve flashed the post together. The bookmakers were convinced that the Irish horse had won, and some of them quoted Hill Society at 10-1 on. As Meade paced nervously in the unsaddling enclosure, people kept coming up to him and telling him he had won. Tony McCoy, the rider of Champleve, took the same view. The one person who saw things differently was Hill Society's jockey, Richard Dunwoody. He told Meade that he was in front a stride before the line and a stride after it, but he feared that he had been headed as he crossed it. It took the judge more than ten minutes to confirm that Dunwoody's version was correct.

In the County Hurdle, the final race of the meeting, Advocat seemed sure to provide compensation when he came to the last almost level with hot favourite Blowing Wind, and apparently going much the better. But the Castletown horse landed awkwardly, lost his momentum and was beaten into second.

No windows were smashed on the journey to the airport, but Meade's ever-present cheerfulness was tested to the limit, and when Cheltenham came up in conversation he sometimes struggled to show a brave face. 'I did think the place had a jinx on me, and those defeats hurt. Of course they did. Nobody ever remembers the ones who were second, and I was annoyed by the press building it all up.'

Luck plays such a part in racing that many people involved in it, whether they be trainers, owners, jockeys or punters, are intensely superstitious. Meade is no exception and his head lad, Paul Cullen, who has worked for the trainer since 1976, is much the same. It was Cullen who told Meade that he should not allow photographers to visit the yard. 'Every time one of our horses is pictured in the papers, something happens to him,' he told his boss. 'We should stop all that.' Meade was only too happy to oblige. He had long since barred journalists and television film crews from watching his horses work.

In the build-up to Cheltenham in 2000, Paul Carberry persuaded him to make an exception. Charlie Brooks was writing an article about the jockey and Carberry said that, as a former trainer, Brooks should be regarded in a different light to the ordinary hack. Brooks looked on as Frozen Groom completed his preparation for the Arkle Trophy by crashing through the first schooling fence and turning a somersault at the third, while the horse's trainer buried his head in his hands in horror.

Whether it was this break with superstition, or some other mysterious reason, the Festival fates finally relented. Sausalito Bay won the opening race of the meeting, his trainer capturing the attention of the photographers as he knelt down in the winner's enclosure in a gesture the Pope would have been proud of. For once, luck had managed to help Meade rather than defeat him. Carberry had cracked a bone in his back three weeks earlier, and he then aggravated the injury in a hunting fall. He rode with a painful blood blister on his back, and this burst shortly after the final hurdle. The pain was so intense that he was unable to do much more than stay on the gelding. Most horses would have responded to the lack of pressure by easing up. Fortunately, Sausalito Bay kept galloping all the way up the hill to the winning post.

The horse who finished second, only three-quarters of a length away, was none other than Best Mate, who was to go on to win three consecutive Cheltenham Gold Cups. Furthermore, Jim Culloty is adamant that the horse would also have won the Supreme Novices' Hurdle that year if he had not given the horse such a bad ride: 'I was boxed in on the inner and I panicked through lack of experience. If I had sat where I was, a gap would have appeared. But I pulled out and ended up coming very wide into the straight. I was suicidal.'

The following day Culloty redeemed himself by winning the Royal & SunAlliance Chase on Lord Noelie. 'I went out to ride him thinking that my future was gone. As a result I gave the horse a very casual ride, and he pissed up!'

Meade's luck did not last long. In the Arkle Trophy, the second race of the meeting, Frozen Groom swept down the hill in the lead travelling like a dream, only to fall at the third last fence. In the following day's Coral Cup Native Dara was well clear jumping the final flight and he headed for the post some eight lengths in front of his nearest pursuer. Just when his trainer was about to turn and run towards the winner's enclosure, Native Dara ran out of steam. He was caught in the last few strides and beaten a neck.

Some five years earlier, when doing his entries for a meeting at The Curragh, it had dawned on Meade that the only races his horses were able to run in were handicaps, where his chances of winning were necessarily slim. They were simply not good enough to run in conditions races, and he resolved to do something about it.

> The Aga Khan and Sheikh Mohammed had come into Ireland in force, and I could see the way Ballydoyle was expanding. I realised that I was never going to get anywhere on the Flat without a major player as an owner. Even if I went to the sales with £100,000, which is quite a lot for any horse, I couldn't buy the ones I wanted. And if you can't compete in the sales ring, you certainly can't do so on the track.
>
> I decided I must concentrate more on the jumpers, and buy more National Hunt types instead of big Flat yearlings that might make jumpers if they didn't prove up to it on the level. If I did this, I felt that I should be able to compete at the highest level, and go to all the top tracks with a winning chance.

Meade continued to train a few Flat horses, but he no longer went to the sales to buy between ten and twenty yearlings each year to sell on when he found clients for them. Instead, he only bought Flat yearlings to order and, as a result, those he purchased tended to be of a higher quality. A notable example was Sunshine Street, who led the field a merry dance in the 1998 Derby and was only caught just before the furlong marker. He finished an honourable fourth and his trainer, who had forsaken his beloved Meath team to go to Epsom, said it was the biggest thrill of his career. The colt was also third in the St Leger.

The first tangible result of the change of policy came the following year when Meade was champion jumps trainer for the first time. He headed the lists for both races won (seventy-seven) and prize money. The next season he was again top for the number of races won but Willie Mullins's horses earned more money. It was the same story in 2000/01 when Mullins headed the prize-money title, and his rival sent out the most winners. However, Meade has topped both lists in every subsequent season.

He achieved a long-standing ambition at Fairyhouse on Easter Monday 2002, when The Bunny Boiler (named by one of the gelding's owners after the character played by Glenn Close in the film *Fatal Attraction*) won the Irish Grand National. The eight-year-old had won the Midlands National at Uttoxeter the previous month, despite not being the most reliable of jumpers, and he came perilously close to blundering away his chance at Fairyhouse with a terrible mistake at the final fence.

Luckily Ross Geraghty, so often overshadowed by his younger brother, sat tight. Meade also had the fourth horse, Arctic Copper, as well as sixth-placed Oa Baldixe. Barry Geraghty, out of luck on Rathbawn Prince, had ridden Arctic Copper at Cheltenham. The gelding was owned by a group of seventeen politicians, including five present or former cabinet ministers. Before he went out to ride the horse in the Cathcart, Geraghty was told by the trainer that the politicians would make him an honorary member of the Dáil if he won. All bar one of the seventeen travelled to Cheltenham to watch the race, but their hopes did not last long. Geraghty was unshipped at the very first fence. As he returned to the weighing room, Meade told him that they had decided to make him an honorary member of Mountjoy instead!

Before Sausalito Bay brought his Cheltenham nightmare to an end, Meade would sometimes console himself by reasoning that, once the first Festival success came, the winners would flow. After all, much the same had happened with other big-name trainers who had trouble breaking the ice at the meeting. The late David Nicholson was a notable example: he had been training for sixteen years before he won the 1986 Triumph Hurdle with Solar Cloud, and two years later he took the Cheltenham Gold Cup with Charter Party. But for Meade there was no such change of fortune. Paul Carberry, by his own admission, fell off Harbour Pilot in the 2002 Royal & SunAlliance Chase, coming in convinced he would have won. It was a painful fall for the stable jockey in more ways than one, because another horse landed on his hand and broke it.

Harbour Pilot ran a fine race to take third in the following year's Gold Cup, and an even better one in the 2004 race when Carberry audaciously attempted to box in Best Mate and nearly succeeded. However, the jockey then went too soon on Harchibald, who was favourite for the County Hurdle, and threw away what looked to be a winning chance.

Only months later did Meade admit that Carberry's uncharacteristic mistake – he might sometimes leave his challenge almost impossibly late, but rarely does he go too soon – was the trainer's fault. 'I was hopping mad over something, and I said to Paul that he had to lie handy. As a result, instead of dropping the horse out, he was fourth or fifth the whole way and, when the leaders fell away, he found himself in front.'

Harchibald, and in particular Carberry's riding of the horse, was the centre of controversy in the 2005 Champion Hurdle. The horse was going best of all at the final flight and his rider sat motionless until fifty yards from the post. When Carberry pressed the button, the gelding found nothing and was beaten a neck. His jockey was booed by a number of disgruntled punters who reckoned he should have gone for his whip, while pundits in the papers and on television argued about whether he should have made his move earlier.

However, Punchestown the following month proved that Carberry had been right to wait as long as he dared. He planned to delay his challenge almost to the line in the Emo Oil Champion Hurdle but Meade, fearing his jockey would get cocky and leave it too late, instructed him to go upsides the leader going down the hill towards the final flight. Harchibald again found little when he came off the bridle, and he was beaten once more.

Sweet Wake started a warm favourite for the 2006 Supreme Novices' Hurdle but, like many fancied Irish horses before him, his reputation had been built on races run on soft ground and at a far from exacting pace. He finished fifth and that evening his trainer, drowning his sorrows with the help of a few gins, vowed never to return to Cheltenham if he did not have a winner the following day. He did not have long to wait. In the first race on the card, the Royal & SunAlliance Novices' Hurdle, Nicanor challenged hotpot Denman at the final flight and powered up the hill in front. Carberry rode into the winner's enclosure with an Irish tricolour wrapped round him and Meade, grinning from ear to ear, declared 'It's magic.'

Sadly, there was no magic about Aran Concerto in the same race twelve months later. This well-bred horse looked a real star in testing conditions at Navan and Leopardstown during the winter, and Meade thought for a time that he just might be the best he had ever trained. He started favourite at Cheltenham but little went right and he made a number of mistakes on the drier ground – it was officially good to soft. When Tony McCoy asked him to quicken, there was nothing left in the tank.

BIGGEST RACES WON

1978
Cork & Orrery Stakes   Sweet Mint

1982
Galway Hurdle   Pinch Hitter

1983
Galway Hurdle   Pinch Hitter

1985
Phoenix Sprint Stakes   Rangoon Ruby

1992
Greenlands Stakes   Street Rebel

1993
Ladbroke Hurdle   Glencloud

1996
Ericsson Chase   Johnny Setaside

1997
AIG Europe Champion Hurdle   Cockney Lad

2000
Supreme Novices' Hurdle   Sausalito Bay

2002
Midlands National   The Bunny Boiler
Irish Grand National   The Bunny Boiler
Paddy Power Handicap Chase   Coq Hardi Diamond

2004
Christmas Hurdle   Harchibald

2005
Galway Hurdle   More Rainbows

2006

Royal & SunAlliance Novices' Hurdle	Nicanor
Christmas Hurdle	Jazz Messenger

10

DERMOT WELD

Melbourne, 2 November 1993. Mick Kinane doffs his helmet, Australian-style, as he rides into the winner's enclosure on the brave but tired Vintage Crop. Expatriate Irishmen yell their appreciation while many of the locals shake their heads in disbelief. They said that it couldn't be done. Yet the Melbourne Cup, the race that stops a nation, has been won for the first time by a horse trained in the Northern Hemisphere.

Dermot Weld served notice that he was going to be a trainer of extraordinary ability when he topped the table in his first year at the age of only twenty-four. He has trained large numbers of winners in every season since, and won an enormous number of big races, over jumps as well as on the Flat. But it is his groundbreaking successes around the globe that mark him apart, and that have earned him a prime place in racing history.

Dermot Charles Kenneth Weld was born in Surrey in 1948, when his father's career as a British-based jump jockey was nearing its close. Charlie Weld and his wife Marguerite, known as Gita, soon moved back to their native Ireland to start training. Their stable's first winner came in 1950 when Tablecloth, partnered by Martin Molony, won a handicap at Roscommon.

Charlie Weld was far more successful as a trainer than he had been as a jockey, and steadily increasing patronage enabled him to move from Phoenix Park to The Curragh where he bought Rosewell House. This yard, little more than a furlong from the winning post of the racecourse, was built by Morny Wing and named after the horse on whom he won the 1938 Irish Derby. Wing trained the 1951 Irish St Leger winner Do Well at Rosewell.

In 1959 Charlie Weld had one of his most important jumping successes when Highfield Lad won the Galway Plate, and the trainer's only son proudly led the horse in to the winner's enclosure. Later that year the stable won the Naas November Handicap with Farney Fox, who showed his versatility by winning the Irish Lincoln at the beginning of the following season. Weld's other major prizes included the 1963 Phoenix Stakes with Right Strath, the Galway Hurdle of two years later with Ticonderoga, both the Irish Cambridgeshire and Cesarewitch (twice), the Ballymoss and Desmond Stakes. The best Flat horse he trained was probably Decies, who won the 1969 National Stakes before being sold to win the following season's Irish 2,000 Guineas for Bernard van Cutsem. Weld never had a classic victory, but in his final season Kingsview was a close third in the Irish 2,000 Guineas.

He did well enough out of training to be able to buy the 240-acre Piper's Hill Stud just outside Naas in 1968. The 1970 Grand National winner Gay Trip had been bred there, and Weld lived at the stud until suffering a fatal heart attack in February 1980. His widow continued to breed horses there, many of them high class and trained by her son.

Charlie was understandably proud of Dermot, who rode his first winner when he was fifteen and still at Newbridge College. In 1964 he won the Players-Wills Amateur Handicap on Ticonderoga. He was to win the big Galway race three times in the 1970s on Spanner, whom he also trained. At just over six feet, Weld was tall for race riding, even for an amateur, and his father expressed amazement at how he tucked himself up like a professional to look almost part of the horse.

Dermot was twenty when he became champion amateur for the first time in 1968. He shared the title with Arthur Moore that year but won it outright two years later, and he repeated the performance in 1971. For part of this time he was studying veterinary medicine at University College, Dublin.

Immediately after I qualified, I decided I would go and study the methods of training, riding and veterinary around the world. The usual system that I had in every country, whether it was in France, America, South Africa or Australia, was to ride work first lot before devoting the rest of the morning to going round the racing stables with a vet, and then I would spend the afternoons with a trainer. That way I had the advantage, not just of studying the methods of one trainer, but of obtaining an insight into those of several.

During this period of his education Weld had one ride in France, one in America and one in South Africa. And he won on all three, including the rank outsider on which he contested the valuable Freight Services Champion Hurdle in South Africa. However, his intention was to practise as a vet rather than train – and to specialise.

It was in Kentucky that my interest in equine surgery really developed. I had the privilege of working with Dr Bob Coplan, one of the greatest horse surgeons in the world, and I thought very hard about coming home and setting up in practice, with the emphasis on equine surgery. But when I did return home, my father decided that he was going to retire early the following year, and I thought that at the time equine surgery on a major scale was not really a financial proposition in Ireland. I spent the remainder of that year, 1971, as assistant to my father. I had originally thought that, if I failed in veterinary, I would train. Now I felt I would try training for a year, and see how I got on.

He started with a string of fifty, all but a handful of them Flat race horses, but he was determined to make an immediate impact. On New Year's Day, his first day with a licence, there was racing at

Baldoyle on the northern outskirts of Dublin, and the new trainer won a hurdle race with Spanner. Later that afternoon he changed into boots and breeches to win the second division of the bumper on Chevy Chase. It was a fantastic start, but few racegoers that day appreciated quite what a talent they were witnessing.

At Leopardstown in early May Weld had his first Pattern winner when Boreen won the Group Two Players-Wills Stakes, and in August he won the Prix Gontaut-Biron at Deauville with the same horse. He gave an early indication of his determination to broaden the accepted racing frontiers by sending Boreen to America to run in the Washington International. Buster Parnell's mount slipped up shortly after halfway, but his trainer's name did not escape the notice of wealthy international owners. And Weld's total of eighty winners in Ireland made him headline news. It was the highest since the legendary Senator Jim Parkinson topped the table with ninety-two in 1926.

Charlie Weld had enjoyed a good season in his final year, sending out forty-two winners and finishing sixth in the trainers' table, but his son was clearly operating on a higher plane. Weld senior did not settle for an easy retirement. He insisted on going out on to the gallops with his son every morning and often went racing with him. He watched the way Dermot was operating and formed his own conclusions about the reasons for his phenomenal success: 'One of the main things is that he is very understanding with his horses – he possesses an innate knowledge of the working of a horse's mind. He also has a knack of only working his horses when they should be worked, and he seems to place them very well. Furthermore, he is dedicated to his job and he is a very hard worker.'

For his part, Weld maintained that he had not set out to do things differently from the way his father had taught him in the previous year, although he tried to combine this with what he had learnt when studying the training methods employed in the various countries he had visited. 'I trained each horse as an individual, and I looked very closely at each horse's mental and psychological attitude, not only towards racing, but towards training as well.' This is more complex than it sounds.

I feel that you must try to understand the mental approach of a horse towards his work, and his racing, and I do endeavour to train them as individuals as well as understand them as individuals. I don't over-work them, and I like them to be relaxed whenever possible. I know my father did this, and so did Tommy Smith in Australia. The methods there differ very much from ours, but one thing that Tommy always did when I was with him was to let his horses graze after they had worked, and then give them a roll in the sand.

If a horse starts leaving his food when you first start working him, you know you have a problem. You have to ask yourself if you are getting him ready too soon, or giving him too much work. It's the same if they start to sweat up before they work. There is always a reason, a psychological reason. They do not do it just because they are over-raced, and you have to find that reason.

Placing them is also of vital importance, placing them where they are not going to be out of their depth, where they are not going to have a hard race first time out against horses who are superior to them. The whole thing amounts to giving them confidence, especially those who are nervous, or those who have a lot of ability but may not wish to produce it, and it's up to you to give them that confidence.

Weld's approach towards the press also marked him out. A trainer in the winner's enclosure has a captive audience only too willing to pass on his or her thoughts and opinions to a wide readership. Some trainers are better at this than others, and gain more publicity as a result. Weld excelled right from that first day at Baldoyle. After speaking about his winner, and without waiting to be asked, he would rattle off the number of winners he had had that year and his plans for the more important members of his string. There was a bit of trumpet-blowing involved but the media give no medals for modesty, false or otherwise. They welcome being given the information they are looking for, and Weld's ability to speak the language of the newspapers paid handsome dividends in terms of press coverage. Training racehorses is a business, and advertising is as important to a trainer as it is to anyone with a service to promote.

Prospective owners were every bit as impressed. They read what the newspapers had to say about the latest training sensation, and listened when he talked to them. Again there was no modesty – he did not hesitate to reel off his record – but they were taken with the confident manner in which he explained what he would be able to achieve with their horses. Where circumstances warranted, he would also tell them how much he could make these horses worth by the time he had finished with them. Weld was soon attracting some of the wealthiest owners in the world. American Bert Firestone sent him horses and so did other big names like Robert Sangster, multi-millionaire Walter Haefner and Ravi Tikkoo, an Indian who had made a fortune out of shipping. When the British government imposed VAT on blood-stock, Tikkoo took six of his best horses away from Scobie Breasley and Ben Hanbury in protest early in 1974, and sent them to Ireland where the government deemed bloodstock to be zero-rated. Tikkoo's move provoked a flood of publicity, all of which benefited the Irish trainer he had selected.

Dermot Weld ensured that Tikkoo did not regret his decision. He turned two of the six into top juveniles, Hot Spark providing the trainer with his first Group One success in the Flying Childers Stakes and Steel Heart winning both the Gimcrack and Middle Park Stakes. Weld also sent out Highest Trump to take the Queen Mary Stakes at Royal Ascot. Firestone's Red Alert won the Jersey Stakes there, and at Goodwood the same horse landed the Stewards' Cup. Weld finished 1974 with 114 winners, including overseas races and those over jumps. His stable was expanding rapidly, both numerically and in terms of quality.

He was still riding in races, although not as often. However, in 1975 he decided to aim Lane Court at the Moet & Chandon Silver Magnum, a race at Epsom held on August Bank Holiday Monday and known as the amateurs' Derby. The colt had won three of his previous four races that season and started second favourite. Weld sent him to the front two and a half furlongs from home, and kept him going to hold Luca Cumani's mount, Fool's Mate, by a length. Four weeks earlier Weld had won the Players-Wills Amateur Handicap for the fourth and final time on the gallant Spanner, who had been successful in both 1972 and 1973.

Two years later the Rosewell House maestro, as some members of the press were referring to him, became the first trainer to send out a century of winners on the Flat in Ireland. His total, including four under National Hunt rules, was 106. Only once had this ever been bettered, in 1923 when Senator Parkinson won 134 races.

However, despite the quality of horses he was now training, it was not until 1981 that Weld won his first classic. Blue Wind had shown herself to be a high-class filly when trained by Paddy Prendergast to win the Silken Glider Stakes at Leopardstown as a two-year-old, and Firestone bought her for 180,000 guineas at Goffs towards the end of the year.

Wally Swinburn was Weld's stable jockey – he also topped the 100-winner mark in 1977 – and he partnered the filly in her first two races in the Firestone colours, including a short head defeat in the Irish 1,000 Guineas. It was widely assumed that he would again have the mount in the Oaks, but Lester Piggott was lurking ominously in the wings, and Blue Wind's owner decided that he should have the mount at Epsom. Piggott sent her clear two furlongs out and she powered home to win by seven lengths, the widest Oaks margin since Noblesse eighteen years earlier.

It was a hugely impressive performance, particularly because the time was more than three seconds faster than Shergar's in the Derby. However, jocking-off Swinburn left a nasty taste in many people's mouths. His son, Walter, had ridden Shergar and a father-and-son classic double would have been supremely popular. In the winner's enclosure the hacks pressed Weld for an explanation. For once, his skills in handling the media went astray. He would only say 'I don't want to comment.' Any form of 'no comment' is invariably taken by the press to be a sign that the person concerned has something to hide. Criticism and unfavourable speculation are the usual consequences and Weld was not given the credit he deserved for his first classic victory. When Swinburn regained the mount in the Irish Oaks, the filly again ran out a convincing winner, although the margin was nothing like so great.

Three years later Weld sent out Saving Mercy to become the first Irish-trained winner of the Lincoln, and he came close to bringing off the spring double when Greasepaint finished second in the Grand National. The nine-year-old had been bought out of Michael Cunningham's stable by multi-millionaire businessman Michael Smurfit, boss of the Smurfit Group, after coming within three-quarters of a length of winning the previous year's National. He started favourite, and for much of the race Tommy Carmody was convinced that his mount was going to win.

> Greasepaint gave me a fantastic ride and everything went right, almost throughout. I left asking him a question as late as possible and, when I did, I felt sure he would find something. But he just kept galloping at the same pace and we were beaten four lengths by Hallo Dandy. It was great to finish second but disappointing not to win. I rode him again the following year and we finished fourth.

That year, 1985, Weld set a new Irish record of 120 Flat winners and his total, including jumping winners, was only two short of Parkinson's 1923 tally. He also had a record nine winners at the Galway Festival and won a second successive Prix de l'Abbaye with Committed.

Back in 1965 Charlie Weld had saddled the favourite for the Irish Grand National, but although there were just four runners owing to an outbreak of coughing, Duke Of York managed only a well-beaten third. Perris Valley put the record straight in 1988, carrying Smurfit's colours and named after the Californian landmark where the owner's son, Tony, did his first parachute jump. However, victory came with an expensive sting in the tail for Weld. In the winner's enclosure he had revealed that he owned half the horse. The Turf Club's registry office staff read the press reports with interest, not least because the partnership was not recorded. Weld was fined £1,000 for what was no more than a clerical error.

Smurfit also owned Rare Holiday, who gave Rosewell House its first Cheltenham Festival winner in the 1990 Triumph Hurdle. The gelding started at 25-1; he had still to win over hurdles and no maiden had won the race for ten years. The 1990 running was a rough race and at least eight of the thirty runners were still in with a chance at the final flight. Rare Holiday was hampered at the third last flight, and on the run-in he caused interference to both the third and fourth before winning by only half a length. The stewards deliberated long and hard, much to the concern of Rare Holiday's owner.

I remember it vividly. Some people said to me 'they won't take it away from you because you are a sponsor', but I knew that was nothing to do with it. In fact, you could argue that the case was quite the opposite because the stewards would bend over backwards to be fair. The result was not decided until the next race had almost started, and as a result we lost that unique atmosphere that really makes a winner at Cheltenham.

Smurfit made a practice of monitoring his racing investment in much the same way as his business operations, while the trainer was assessed as if he was one of the executives in the Smurfit Group.

I get a regular report on what each horse is costing me to run, and I get a printout every month or two. I accept that most of it produces solid red figures, except in the rare year when you win something like the Derby or the Melbourne Cup, but if I were in racing for money I wouldn't be in it at all. I just want to be sure that I know what I am losing rather than be somebody that doesn't care. I do care. It's hard enough to earn money without throwing it away.

I also take the view that horses are there to be raced, not just to eat and enjoy the comforts of the stable. Trainers tend to baby their horses whereas the nature of the owner is that he wants them to race. In my experience a lot of trainers run their horses too little, and Dermot Weld tends to be on the cautious side. He and I had regular chats about this!

Less than three months after Rare Holiday's Cheltenham victory came a far more important achievement. Weld had harboured notions about having a crack at an American classic since his educational stint in the States, where the courses at which he worked included Belmont Park in New York, and it was in the Belmont Stakes that he made racing history in June 1990.

The previous October, Go And Go had made a successful trip to Washington for the Laurel Futurity, a race that was considered suitable for European-trained horses because it was run on grass. After torrential rain flooded the course, the race had to be switched to the adjoining dirt track, but Go And Go still managed to win, and although he disappointed in the Breeders' Cup Juvenile on a similar surface a fortnight later, the colt's poor performance was thought to be due to the stifling heat in the barns.

Weld's plan the following year was to train Go And Go for the Derby but, after he managed only fourth in the Derrinstown Stud Derby Trial, that ambition was shelved in favour of a tilt at the Belmont Stakes. The race is the final leg of the American Triple Crown, and although it took less winning than the Blue Riband at

Epsom it was nevertheless an ambitious target. Yet Mick Kinane's mount left the home-trained opposition for dead in the final furlong, drawing right away to win by over eight lengths. Comparatively few European-trained horses had ever run in an American classic, although in the previous year Patrick-Louis Biancone's Le Voyageur finished third in the Belmont and in 1986 Clive Brittain's Bold Arrangement was second in the Kentucky Derby. But to win a leg of the Triple Crown was remarkable by any standards. Some newspapers even likened Weld to Christopher Columbus.

At the end of 1991 the master of Rosewell House did it again, becoming the first European-based trainer to win a race in Hong Kong. He flew out Additional Risk, owned like Go And Go by Walter Haefner's Moyglare Stud Farm and ridden by Kinane, to win the Invitation Bowl. There was some doubt about the status of the race: the Hong Kong authorities regarded it as a Group One event but the European Pattern Committee did not recognise it as such, and it went down in some form books as a Listed race. But this hardly detracted from the merit of the achievement.

The best was still to come. If Weld's American ambitions had been nurtured by the time he spent working on the racetracks there, so his desire to win the Melbourne Cup had been inspired by the months he worked for Tommy Smith. He thought he had the right horse for the race in 1992 in Vintage Crop, a tough gelding who had to overcome persistent back problems later in his career, but quarantine restrictions made a challenge almost impossibly demanding, and the considerable cost of the trip was also a significant factor.

However, the Victoria Racing Club's enthusiastic race promoter, Les Benton, was every bit as keen as Weld for Vintage Crop to run in Australia's most famous race, and VRC officials were persuaded to visit Ireland during the summer of 1993 to make the quarantine regulations more suitable for overseas challengers. They agreed to split the statutory four-week period into two, the first fortnight being spent in the home country. Michael Smurfit's gelding paid for his fare (plus those of his owner, trainer and jockey) several times over by winning £87,600 in the Irish St Leger, sponsored by the Smurfit Group. Amazingly, the tough six-year-old had begun the year by running in the Champion Hurdle (also Smurfit Group-sponsored). He also contested the Ascot Gold Cup.

Weld had spent more than a year cajoling airfreight officials into putting on transport that would not involve long stopovers. Even so, it took Vintage Crop thirty-eight hours to travel the 10,000 miles from Dublin to Melbourne, where the horse was stabled at an isolation centre on the outskirts of the city. As reports of weight loss, caused by the gruelling journey, spread, so the horse drifted in the betting while the locals poured scorn on his preparation. Most Australian trainers believed that it was impossible for a horse to win their greatest race without having a preliminary in the previous ten days. But Smurfit had faith in the horse and his trainer, backing this up to the tune of £10,000. 'I generally only bet to cover the expenses of a dinner party, but I started backing Vintage Crop after he was beaten in the Meld Stakes at The Curragh in August.'

Kinane's mount started at 14-1 with the still disbelieving local bookmakers and he made a poor start. He found himself crowded among the backmarkers, and the way his ears went back showed how much he disliked the Australian style of close riding. His jockey had to drive him to get into a decent position. Kinane feared that some of the Aussie jocks would try to 'take me out', and he moved off the rails to give himself more room. Rounding the final turn a sod of earth hit Vintage Crop in the face. For a stride, he faltered, but he bravely responded to Kinane's every call to hit the front inside the final furlong and win going away. It was the first time that the Melbourne Cup had been won by a horse trained outside Australia or New Zealand, as well as the first occasion that a Northern Hemisphere-trained horse had won a major race in the Southern Hemisphere.

The local racing press, most of them even more hard-bitten than their European counterparts, were taken aback when the winning trainer told them that he had had a love of Australia since childhood, and that this was inspired by Banjo Paterson's book *The Man From Snowy River*. He promptly began quoting verses from it.

Before he left for Ireland, Weld was presented with a key to the City of Melbourne to mark his achievement. He is convinced that his amazing victory brought about a sea change in attitudes among racing authorities throughout the world:

> Most countries had been negative towards foreign horses coming in and winning their prize money. Vintage Crop's win made them realise all the positive effects of an overseas horse winning, not only from the publicity angle but from almost every other point of view. The worldwide prestige of the race would be enhanced, together with its appeal, and that of the country's racing. There are also tourism benefits.

After crediting his owner with nearly £600,000 sterling, Vintage Crop was never asked to risk his neck over hurdles again, but he went back to Australia for the next two Melbourne Cups. In 1994 he started favourite but had no luck in running and finished seventh. The Australian media were almost universal in blaming Kinane for going too wide – 'the Irishman covered more ground than the early explorers' – but horse and rider finished an honourable third in 1995.

Despite the history-making overseas successes, there was no let-up on the home front. Jim Parkinson's 1923 record of 134 winners finally fell in 1990 when Jim Bolger sent out 148 winners in Ireland, and the following year Weld beat this figure by two. The new record lasted for only three years. In 1994 Aidan O'Brien, in a manner reminiscent of the legendary senator, swept almost all before him to clock up a total of 176. O'Brien put even this in the shade in 1995 when he won 241 of the 1,736 races run in Ireland, almost one race in seven.

One of the few big prizes in Ireland to elude Rosewell House was the Irish Derby, although there were some near misses. Theatrical was second in 1985, and Definite Article was beaten no more than the width of a betting slip ten years later. Victory finally came in 1996 in the unlikely form of Zagreb (a son of Theatrical), who started at 20-1 after being beaten on his previous start in a minor race at Leopardstown and rejected by Kinane. Pat Shanahan, who rode Weld's second and third strings for much of his career, made the most of his opportunity to partner the colt to a six-length victory. Zagreb, ante-post favourite for the Arc after this runaway win, flopped in Paris and never ran again. But his trainer has fond memories of him.

> He was a difficult horse to train, and a difficult horse to keep right mentally, but he had always shown me brilliance, and when he won his maiden on his debut as a three-year-old he annihilated a field of twenty-seven. He was inconsistent but he was very talented, and on his day a brilliant horse. When he produced that great acceleration to go away early in the straight in the Irish Derby, I was not in the least surprised.

Victory completed a full hand of the five Irish classics for Weld, and the following month he also won the Irish Oaks with Dance Design.

Unlike most other top Flat trainers, Weld has tutored his jockeys as effectively as his horses. It is the practice of most leading trainers to appoint stable jockeys from among the finest riders, and then try to work with them as best they can. Weld ensures that they do it his way. Mick Kinane, who held the post for fifteen years, was brought in Sunday after Sunday when he joined the stable in order to study videos of races he had ridden. He was told what he had done right and what he had done wrong, as well as the way he should do it in future. His successor, Pat Smullen, was subjected to the same educational process. The Weld method is normally to sit handy until approaching the furlong marker. Some horses are better suited making the running, or being dropped out, but the vast majority of Rosewell House runners are ridden to the trainer's standard procedure. He hates to see jockeys going to the front too soon, and races being lost through leaving it too late. His method has the considerable advantage of ensuring that mistakes are kept to a minimum.

Throughout his career Weld has put the Galway Festival high on his list of priorities, and he has an extraordinary fondness for the two-year-old maiden race on the opening evening of the meeting. He won this in his first season with the subsequent Royal Ascot winner Klairvimy, and year after year he prepared what would often turn out to be a very good colt. Go And Go won it in 1989, as did Grey Swallow in 2003. Aidan O'Brien, Jim Bolger, John Oxx and Kevin Prendergast have sometimes produced a better two-year-old for the race, but normally the Weld runner wins.

His horses have an incredible following at Galway and invariably start at short prices. In 1993, when his tally reached double figures for the first time, he also sent out no fewer than twelve beaten favourites, and he again went home with ten winners in 1994, 1998 and 2001. He won the Galway Plate first in 1990 with Kiichi (winner of the Monday evening two-year-old race three years earlier), and then in 1993 with General Idea. Ansar won the big chase in 2004 and repeated the performance twelve months later, and he also won the Galway Hurdle in 2001.

When Senator Jim Parkinson – who came from Tramore and qualified as a vet before taking up training, and who had one of the biggest strings in Europe for much of a career that lasted for almost half a century – died in 1948, he had registered 2,577 winners in Ireland. Weld reached this long sought-after figure on the final day of the 2000 Galway Festival, and he passed it when Georgia Peach won at Naas the following day.

It was a memorable occasion, and Weld promptly spoke of reducing the size of his string. 'I am thinking of cutting back by a third. I believe I can do a better job with fewer horses. Also, I value my life and my health.' The cynics among his rivals, and in the racecourse pressrooms, gave a wry smile. Weld had talked for years of cutting down the numbers, but there was precious little evidence of it. For example, in 1994 he ran 153 horses on the Flat alone. In 2000 he ran 134, but four years later the figure was back to over 150.

Weld added another notable international race to his personal roll of honour in 2000 when Pine Dance won the American Derby. This nine and a half furlong event, run at Arlington Park in Chicago, is perhaps not as important as its name suggests because it carries only a Grade Two tag. However, it was still a significant scalp, and Weld also won it with Evolving Tactics in 2003 and Simple Exchange the following year.

The real achievement, though, came once more in Australia's most famous race. In some ways it is even more difficult for a European-trained horse to win the Melbourne Cup than any of the big races in America because it is a handicap. In theory, every horse in the race has an equal chance but the Australian trainers target it for years ahead, and some of them make sure that their horses stay a few pounds ahead of the handicapper.

In 2002 Weld's main hope was Vinnie Roe, a horse in the mould of Vintage Crop. He was never asked to race over hurdles – not least because he was an entire horse, whereas Vintage Crop was a gelding – but he won the Irish St Leger four years in succession. Weld also sent out Media Puzzle, a gelding by Theatrical and bred by Moyglare before being sold to Smurfit.

Media Puzzle was far from certain to make the cut for the Melbourne Cup, so he ran in a race at Geelong just under a fortnight before the big race in the hope that he would win and pick up a penalty. Not only did he do so but he thrived in the sunshine, whereas Vinnie Roe took time to put back the weight he lost on the long journey. Such was their trainer's reputation by this stage that Vinnie Roe started favourite and Media Puzzle was the next best-backed horse. And he won in the second-fastest time in the long history of the Melbourne Cup, while Vinnie Roe finished fourth under top weight.

Two years later Vinnie Roe was second to wonder horse Makybe Diva with Media Puzzle unplaced, and in 2005 Vinnie Roe finished eighth behind the great mare with his trainer firmly established as the supreme master of the complicated art of winning major overseas prizes.

> Winning such races is never easy, but it should be slightly easier now than it was at the time of Vintage Crop's Melbourne Cup because flight times have slightly shortened and quarantine facilities have been improved. However, the one thing that has not changed is the stress of travelling. As with humans, a lot of horses do not travel well – it is extremely tiring for them – and the name of the game is picking the right ones.

Weld and his wife Mary – they married in November 1972 – have two sons. Mark, a qualified pilot and a brilliant singer, often represents his father when the horses run in big races abroad, and Kris is keen to follow in his father's footsteps when he has finished his education. The boys are heirs to a considerable fortune. Weld, like his father before him, has put the money he has earned from training to good use. He bought Rathbride, where Mick Rogers trained Derby winners Hard Ridden and Santa Claus, following Rogers's death in 1985 and more recently he has set about turning parts of Piper's Hill Stud into a business park.

His mother still breeds high-class horses, notably the 2004 Irish Derby winner Grey Swallow and the 2006 Irish 1,000 Guineas heroine, Nightime, and they have provided an important stimulus: 'Training horses is a very tough profession, and to stay at the top you need to have good horses. It's a seven-day week job, more so now than ever before, and you need the top horses to keep you sane.'

Weld has been Ireland's champion Flat race trainer nine times and has headed the lists for races won on twenty-one occasions. He has one further overseas ambition. Winning a race in South Africa would make him the first to train a winner on all five continents, and for some time he has been eyeing the J & B Met in Cape Town. So far disease has thwarted him. The racing authorities, keen to attract the Maktoums as well as trainers like Weld, have built a quarantine station in the middle of Kenilworth racecourse, but after repeated outbreaks of African horse sickness the European Union has imposed periodic bans on horses flying in and out of South Africa. Even when the bans have been lifted, the restrictions have been such that it has not been possible for the Met to attract runners from Europe. But Weld is still determined to win a race in South Africa, even if it's not the Met, and he has been exploring the possibility of sending two or three horses out there towards the end of 2007.

BIGGEST RACES WON

1974
Flying Childers	Hot Spark
Middle Park Stakes	Steel Heart

1977
National Stakes	Diamonds Are Trump
Cheveley Park Stakes	Sookera

1978
Phoenix Stakes	Kilijaro
Coronation Stakes	Sutton Place

1979
Phoenix Stakes   Smokey Lady

1981
Oaks   Blue Wind
Irish Oaks   Blue Wind
National Stakes   Day Is Done

1982
Irish 1,000 Guineas   Prince's Polly

1984
William Hill Sprint Championship   Committed
Prix de l'Abbaye   Committed

1985
Premio Parioli   Again Tomorrow
Galway Hurdle   Strathline
Prix de l'Abbaye   Committed

1986
Irish 2,000 Guineas   Flash Of Steel

1987
Moyglare Stud Stakes   Flutter Away

1988
Premio Parioli   Gay Burslem
Irish Grand National   Perris Valley
Irish 1,000 Guineas   Trusted Partner

1989
Cartier Million   The Caretaker

1990

Triumph Hurdle	Rare Holiday
Belmont Stakes	Go And Go
Cartier Million	Rinka Das
Galway Plate	Kiichi

1991

Hong Kong Invitation Bowl	Additional Risk

1992

Italian Derby	In A Tiff
St James's Palace Stakes	Brief Truce

1993

Galway Plate	General Idea
Bayerisches Zuchtrennen	Market Booster
Irish St Leger	Vintage Crop
Melbourne Cup	Vintage Crop

1994

AIG Europe Champion Hurdle	Fortune And Fame
Irish St Leger	Vintage Crop
National Stakes	Definite Article

1995

AIG Europe Champion Hurdle	Fortune And Fame

1996

Irish Derby	Zagreb
Irish Oaks	Dance Design

1998

National Stakes	Mus-If

2001
Galway Hurdle	Ansar
Irish St Leger	Vinnie Roe
Prix Royal-Oak	Vinnie Roe

2002
National Stakes	Refuse To Bend
Irish St Leger	Vinnie Roe
Melbourne Cup	Media Puzzle
Matriarch Stakes	Dress To Thrill

2003
2,000 Guineas	Refuse To Bend
Irish St Leger	Vinnie Roe
Flower Bowl Invitational Stakes	Dimitrova

2004
Irish Derby	Grey Swallow
Galway Plate	Ansar
Irish St Leger	Vinnie Roe

2005
Tattersalls Gold Cup	Grey Swallow
Galway Plate	Ansar

2006
Irish 1,000 Guineas	Nightime

11

DAVID WACHMAN

Widely regarded as the Ballydoyle heir apparent, David Wachman spent much of his first six years as a trainer in comparative obscurity, proving himself the hard way. His marriage to John Magnier's daughter has brought him into the limelight and transformed the quality of horse he trains, but he has shown that he has what it takes to make it at the top level by winning big races for owners other than his father-in-law.

The Wachmans came to Ireland from Poland, and in 1935 David's grandfather set up the Edenderry Shoe Company, which from small beginnings became a major supplier to the footwear industry. The factory was also a boon to the poor County Offaly town that was otherwise an unemployment blackspot, but at times it struggled to cope with the lack of prosperity prevalent almost throughout the country before the advent of the Celtic Tiger, the dramatic trans-formation of the Irish economy. In 1984, for instance, the Wachmans were forced to put their workers on a three-day week. By 1987, when there were 150 people on the payroll, the majority of the shares had been sold to an investment bank. When the factory closed four years later, the workforce numbered fewer than 100.

David, who was born in July 1971, grew up in the picturesque village of Carbury, only a few miles from the straggling and rather bleak town where his father worked. His parents were well off, certainly by local standards. There were ponies and hunters on the property, and David was sent to Glenstal, the boys' public school run by Benedictine monks at Moroe in County Limerick. However, he had no wish to follow his father and grandfather into the shoe business, and his heart was set on becoming a trainer well before he left school. As a result of his friendship with Jessica Harrington's son, James, he was invited to stay at her stables in Moone during the school holidays. The teenager rode out with the string and helped in the yard, loving every moment of it.

He resolved to learn the trade by working for trainers in different parts of the world. When he left school, he went to Australia and got a job with Bill Mitchell at Randwick in Sydney. After a year, he flew home and went to work for Jenny Pitman in Lambourn. Then it was back to Ireland to join Jim Bolger. Twelve months later he returned to Australia, this time to work for Brian Mayfield-Smith. His final understudy stint lasted the longest, three years with Michael Hourigan. It was a thorough grounding: 'Jenny Pitman's attention to detail was very high, and her standard of stable management was excellent – and her bark was worse than her bite! I learned more about training racehorses from Jim Bolger than from anyone else, and during my time with Michael Hourigan I learned a lot about the economics of the business.'

Many of those who turn to training do so after making a name for themselves riding in races, but Wachman had no such advantage. He had a few rides in point-to-points but he never rode a winner: 'I had difficulty keeping the horse between myself and the ground.' Finding owners was going to be just as problematical. A tall man, he comes across as a serious individual. While he gives the impression of being a sound, sensible character who can be relied upon to do what he says he will, he does not have the bubbly, enthusiastic personality that easily attracts owners.

However, he had made a lot of contacts by the time he applied for a trainer's licence in 1996, and enough of them agreed to put horses with him to satisfy the Turf Club's licensing committee. The minimum requirement is six horses, and Wachman had this half dozen, all National Hunt, as well as the promise of two two-year-olds for the following year. As he did not have the money to buy his own premises, he made an arrangement to lease a yard of twenty-three boxes at South Lodge, on the main road between Clonmel and Kilkenny. A famous training establishment in the days when it was owned by Phonsie O'Brien and later by Adrian Maxwell, South Lodge had a much quieter time after Maxwell split up with his wife and moved to America. Ger Hourigan, who had bought it, did not have enough horses to fill all the boxes, and so it suited him to sublet one of the yards.

Wachman had some early point-to-point winners, and he went within inches of making a dream start on the racecourse when Middle Moggs was caught on the line in a bumper at Naas. At Clonmel, three races and six weeks later, the four-year-old filly made amends by getting up close to home to win a maiden hurdle. Wachman had to wait six months for his next winner, but Vital Issue's success in a bumper at Listowel was of considerable significance. The newcomer was owned by Paul Shanahan, a key member of the Coolmore organisation and one of John Magnier's right-hand men. Some of the other Coolmore executives were sufficiently impressed to send Wachman horses over the next few years. The new boy finished the 1996/97 season with five winners, four of them in bumpers.

I was lucky that first year in that the horses stayed healthy. That is the key: if the horses are healthy they can run to their optimum, no matter how bad they are. I didn't have much capital when I started, and I bought store horses with what I had. I kept a stake in many of those that won and I then got them sold. If they hadn't clicked, it would have been a different ball game. Even so, starting off was difficult and that first year was tricky.

The two-year-olds he was promised duly materialised, and both of them won – Clewbay Pearl at Cork and Bombay Mix twice at Sligo. Bombay Mix was owned by the trainer's uncle, Nick Wachman, who later became a steward of the Turf Club.

Wachman reinvested his share of the sale money in more store horses. Many of these also did enough to enable them to be sold at a profit, and less than three years after he started training he was doing sufficiently well to be able to buy a small farm a mile away from South Lodge, and build forty boxes there. He attracted enough horses not only to fill them all, but also to justify continuing the lease on the yard at South Lodge.

At the Tralee festival in August 2000 he had his first Listed winner when Rush Brook won the Ruby Stakes, and it was at about this time that the racecourse grapevine picked up that he was dating Katie Magnier. According to the gossip-mongers, he was made for life if the relationship progressed to marriage, and doomed if he was the one to break it off. As with most gossip, there was a fair amount of exaggeration involved, but what the storytellers meant was that John Magnier would be sure to send top quality horses to any trainer son-in-law, and that he is such a powerful and influential figure that few owners would want to send horses to anyone who upset the family.

Magnier himself was educated at Glenstal but left when he was sixteen. After his father died, his mother needed him to help run the family's Grange Stud near Fermoy in County Cork. The Magniers have been breeding racehorses, and standing stallions, for many generations and Thomas (John's grandfather) had the famous Edlington. This horse, after winning fourteen races in the 1880s, was what was called a travelling stallion, being led and ridden from farm to farm to cover thoroughbred mares in Cork and neighbouring counties. John's father, Michael, stood a number of highly successful National Hunt sires at the Grange Stud, including Fortina, Cottage and Even Money.

Even as a teenager, John Magnier promised to be rather more than a chip off the old block, and he soon put into action some ambitious plans for expansion. These embraced the purchase of the 200-acre Castle Hyde Stud to add to the 300 acres at nearby Grange. The latter continued to house jumping sires, while Magnier used Castle Hyde for the Flat stallions he was buying into.

In 1973 Vincent O'Brien bought two-thirds of Coolmore Stud, just outside the County Tipperary town of Fethard and then standing on 400 acres, from Tim Vigors. The bloodstock agent and former Battle of Britain wing commander was involved in an expensive divorce settlement and needed the money. O'Brien asked Magnier to manage Coolmore. Before long, the stud was amalgamated with Castle Hyde, and was expanded further as Magnier increased the numbers of stallions to embrace high-class horses that had been trained by O'Brien.

By 1975, when Magnier married O'Brien's daughter Sue, Vernons Pools boss Robert Sangster was also a partner in the O'Brien–Magnier racehorse/stallion business. They bought the best yearlings in the world, usually at Keeneland in Kentucky, trained them at Ballydoyle and stood the most successful of them at Coolmore. These earned many times their purchase price and training costs in stud fees, which were tax free in Ireland.

Magnier made the operation even more profitable by sweeping aside long-established breeding assumptions and principles. It had long been accepted that a top Flat stallion should be syndicated among forty shareholders, each one a breeder who would have the right to send a mare to the horse. Maybe a few extra mares would be accepted to meet the costs of keeping the stallion, but he would not be asked to cover more than forty-five mares. Magnier steadily increased the number covered by the Coolmore stallions to around a hundred, while the total for the National Hunt stallions in their much longer season would sometimes reach three hundred. Traditionalists threw up their hands in horror and many were extremely critical. Some of the bloodstock experts in the newspapers were equally condemnatory. However, the improved veterinary and fertility methods developed at Coolmore meant that the majority of the mares went into foal on only one covering, whereas it often took several matings in the forty-five-book days.

Magnier also decided to make profitable use of the long idle period between mating seasons by flying the Flat stallions to Australia and New Zealand, where the mares are covered in September, October and November. He had them back in Ireland in time for the 15 February start date of the Northern Hemisphere season. In addition, he established an American branch of Coolmore at the Ashford Stud in Kentucky for those stallions that had more appeal to American breeders. In less than twenty years he turned Coolmore from an ordinary Irish stud into the stallion capital of the world, making himself a multi-millionaire in the process.

Like most business tycoons, Magnier works hard and seldom takes much time off. Even when he is abroad on holiday, he is on the phone to Coolmore each day. His success has brought a certain amount of envy and resentment, particularly because his essentially shy manner can give the impression that he is being offhand. But those who work for Coolmore will not have a bad word said about him. He has encouraged them to take a stake in the bloodstock business by buying mares or foals, and many have profited handsomely from his advice. Just as significantly, those who have left his employment to run studs of their own also hold him in high esteem.

Most of the criticism now tends to come from newspapers, particularly from non-racing journalists who resent the aura of secrecy that often seems to surround the man. Such reporters' approach inevitably hardens when Magnier refuses to take their telephone calls. Racing journalists get no further with him on the phone, but on the racecourse he will talk, even if his reply to questions often begins, 'Listen, you didn't get this from me, but . . .'

Magnier hates personal publicity, and he seldom makes speeches or public pronouncements. For several years he was a member of Seanad

Éireann, Ireland's upper house. He was appointed by the Taoiseach, yet he hardly ever spoke in the chamber. One of his few public utterances came in April 2000, long after he had left the Seanad, when the Turf Club was dragging its feet over the government's offer of new funding for racing. Speaking at the Irish Thoroughbred Breeders' Awards dinner, at which he was inducted into the ITBA Hall of Fame, he launched a blistering attack on the Turf Club of which he is a member.

> We have two ministers [Charlie McCreevy, Minister for Finance, and Agriculture Minister Joe Walsh] who have offered to set up racing's finances in perpetuity. We are being given this extraordinary lifeline. Why are we not saying yes to it? Unless everybody in this room first wakes up, and then stands up, a handful of amateurs – and by that I mean people who do not rely on this business for their living – are going to cost professional trainers, jockeys, breeders, agents, stable staff and a mass of others their livelihoods. To be blunter still, there is a very small minority refusing to co-exist with government, and never before have the decisions of so few amateurs affected so many professionals.

Magnier got more than he bargained for when he bought a large slice of Manchester United, as did his fellow Cubic Expression investor, the equally publicity-shy J.P. McManus. Both men were subjected to an enormous amount of press intrusion, particularly as their investment coincided with the row with United manager Sir Alex Ferguson over the ownership of Rock Of Gibraltar. Magnier and McManus eventually sold their shares at a massive profit, but all the publicity left a nasty taste in their mouths.

One of Magnier's few non-racing interests is his collection of works of art, particularly paintings by famous artists. He has managed to build up one of the finest private collections in the world without attracting adverse publicity, even though the identity of the purchaser invariably leaks out when notable paintings make large sums at auction.

Magnier was well aware that his daughter's wedding would give the gossip columnists a field day, but Katie has an understandably special place in his affections and he was determined to make her day an occasion to remember. The wedding is reported to have cost €3 million, and the guest list was made up of a veritable Who's Who. Those from the entertainment world included Lord (Andrew) Lloyd Webber and Michael Flatley, while Joe Walsh, Charlie McCreevy and former Taoiseach Albert Reynolds were among the politicians. Ryanair boss Michael O'Leary was there, as were financier Dermot Desmond, model Jodie Kidd, Sir Alex Ferguson and Ladbrokes' Mike Dillon. Magnier and his wife also invited a number of local people, as well as some of the staff at Coolmore – where there was a marquee so big that it covered several trees.

The service was held on the evening of Saturday, 24 August 2002 in the Augustinian abbey on the outskirts of Fethard. A number of the overseas guests stayed at the luxurious Mount Juliet Hotel in County Kilkenny and were ferried to Coolmore by helicopters and chauffeur-driven cars. They were treated to acrobats swinging from the ceiling of the marquee, and to performances by Rod Stewart and Ronan Keating. If the thirty-one-year-old grandson of Polish immigrants was bemused by all this, he gave no sign of it.

Magnier's generosity went far beyond the lavish ceremony. His wedding present to the couple was the Longfield Stud, 340 acres of prime Tipperary land plus stabling and a character-filled house built by Carlo Bianconi in the second half of the nineteenth century. Bianconi, who came to Ireland from Lombardy, was an enterprising individual who made a fortune out of public transport. He began with one horse-drawn carriage in 1815, taking passengers between Cahir and Clonmel. Within a decade he was operating throughout Munster and south Leinster, his carriages taking up to twenty people a time. When the advent of the railway posed a threat to his business, he switched his routes to take people to the stations and, hedging his bets, bought shares in the railway companies.

Longfield, six miles from Cashel and bordered by the River Suir, is a picturesque place. The new incumbent had been there as a teenager: the monks at Glenstal had organised an outing for some of the boys, not least because one of the resident stallions was named after the school. David Wachman remembers meeting Tommy Stack, who was managing the stud and training a couple of horses under permit.

Wachman's father-in-law may have given the newlyweds the stud, but it was up to them to turn it into a training establishment. The couple moved in on their return from honeymoon and set about building an indoor school as well as gallops, both grass and all-weather. The latter was made of the same state-of-the-art rubber and sand mix installed by Jonjo O'Neill at McManus's Jackdaws Castle in Gloucestershire, and the many grass gallops include one stretch of ten furlongs. Wachman even bought an acre of land from his next-door neighbour so that the gallops could stretch as far as he wanted.

The horses at Wachman's old place near South Lodge were moved in, and the following spring Knock Knock was pipped on the post by Timbera in the Irish Grand National. It was a heartbreaking near miss for the horse's trainer, particularly as the six-year-old would almost certainly have won had he not made a terrible mistake early on the final circuit. 'He was a novice, and he made a novicey mistake,' Wachman ruefully reflected. 'It shuffled him back to last and it cost him the race.'

The trainer could have chosen the move to Longfield as an opportunity to concentrate solely on the Flat, but he continued to train jumpers as well, and he is emphatic that this is the way he wants to go on.

I enjoy the jumpers, and I like having a mixture between Flat and National Hunt because it means that there is always something coming up, always a bunch of horses coming through, whether it's jumpers or two-year-olds. It's not as if you have to wait until the following season for the next lot to race. You can forget about yesterday and concentrate on tomorrow.

That year, 2003, Wachman had twenty-four winners on the Flat in Ireland. It was the first time he had reached double figures in a season, and he finished in the top ten. He also had his first Group success when Venturi, owned by Paul Shanahan, won the C.L. Weld Park Stakes.

Shortly before her marriage, Katie publicly expressed the hope that her father would send David some decent horses to train. Magnier did not disappoint her, and in 2004 several choice-bred fillies began their racing careers at Longfield. One of these was Damson, who cost €160,000 as a yearling even though her sire, the 1997 2,000 Guineas winner Entrepreneur, had fallen so far out of fashion that he had been sold by Coolmore to stand in Russia.

Damson won on her debut at Cork on Easter Monday, and eight weeks later she ran out the easy winner of a Listed race at Naas. With the Queen Mary Stakes at Royal Ascot only nine days away, Wachman scotched press suggestions that she might take her chance. The race came too soon, he said, after pausing a fraction as he often does when answering a question.

I was always going to enter her and have a look, even though I told the press I wasn't going to run. She had plenty of pace, and although they went a good gallop in the Swordlestown Stud Sprint Stakes, she was never out of a half-speed. She came out of that race well, and when I looked at what was in the Queen Mary I thought she could win. It didn't look a great race and there didn't appear anything outstanding in it, certainly nothing like Queen's Logic or Lyric Fantasy. I felt I had nothing to lose by running her, and there was no great pressure on me. I would have been disappointed if she hadn't won, but it was not as if she was a stand-out bet in the eyes of everybody else.

There were eight other previous winners in the race, yet Damson, a strong and sturdy-looking filly, started joint favourite. Jamie Spencer gave her trainer some anxious moments by dropping her right out – 'he told me that he was going to take his time, but after the first 200 yards I was concerned that she was so far back' – but she produced a devastating turn of foot when Spencer asked her to quicken at the two furlong marker. She weaved her way through the field, hit the front just inside the furlong pole and came away to win easily.

The 2004 season was Aidan O'Brien's annus horribilis, when his number of Group One winners dropped to a mere three. He had had only one by the time of the Royal meeting, when the rumour-mongers were saying that he was about to be sacked. Wachman's name had already been mentioned as a replacement and his Queen Mary success fuelled the fire – as did O'Brien himself, who was only too aware of the stories. When he finally got his first winner of the meeting the following day, he told the assembled press corps, 'That'll give me another month or two before David Wachman comes and gets me!'

O'Brien had his tongue only partly in his cheek: he knew that he had to achieve Group One results if he was to retain the confidence of John Magnier and Michael Tabor. But in the Phoenix Stakes at The Curragh in August the pressure was more on his mooted replace-ment. O'Brien had four winners that day and earned glowing praise from Magnier for bringing One Cool Cat back to form, yet for once there was no great expectation on him in the big race. He ran two of the six runners, but Damson was odds-on and Wachman was looking even more serious than usual.

Damson did not produce the same electrifying burst that had left the opposition for dead at Ascot, but she did enough to become the first filly to win the Phoenix Stakes for ten years, and give her trainer his first Group One victory. Far from expressing delight, Wachman admitted that his principal reaction was one of relief.

The filly never won again. She started at odds-on for her next race, the Cheveley Park at the end of September, but she could only manage third. She picked up an infection when sent back to Newmarket for the 1,000 Guineas the following spring, before briefly flattering only to disappoint in the Irish version. Two further below-par efforts established that she had failed to train on, and she was retired. But at least her trainer had proved to his father-in-law that he could achieve success at the highest level if he was given the raw material.

Though 2005 might not have been Damson's year, it saw Wachman strengthen his reputation, particularly as several of his big race successes were not in the dark blue colours of his in-laws. With Michael Nolan's Indesatchel he won both the Loughbrown and the Tetrarch Stakes at The Curragh, as well as the Greenham Stakes at Newbury. Fracas, owned by wealthy builder Joseph Joyce, won the Sandown Classic Trial and the Derrinstown Stud Derby Trial Stakes before finishing a creditable fourth at Epsom.

The only one of the stable's Group winners with a Magnier link was Luas Line. This filly carried the colours of Evie Stockwell, the Coolmore boss's mother, and she won three successive races including the Grade One Garden City Breeders' Cup Handicap in New York.

A virus played havoc with Wachman's hopes for the first half of 2006, also leaving its mark in the remainder of the season, but he made a flying start to 2007 and in June added to his Group race tally with Liscanna in the Ballyogan Stakes. However, he has already achieved enough to suggest that he will be a key player for the rest of his career, particularly because his father-in-law seems sure to go on sending him well-bred horses year after year. Indeed, the Magnier connection makes Wachman the obvious choice to succeed O'Brien at Ballydoyle, assuming the day eventually comes when the present occupant decides to set up on his own.

Wachman has always tried to play down suggestions that he might one day take over ('it's all pub talk'), but he is not short of ambition.

He says that he wants to 'keep increasing the quality of the horses, and I would like to win all the big races'. *All* of them might be over-ambitious, but he has time on his side and he should win many.

BIGGEST RACES WON

2003
C.L. Weld Park Stakes   Venturi

2004
Queen Mary Stakes   Damson
Phoenix Stakes   Damson

2005
Loughbrown Stakes   Indesatchel
Tetrarch Stakes   Indesatchel
Greenham Stakes   Indesatchel
Sandown Classic Trial   Fracas
Derrinstown Stud Derby Trial   Fracas
Garden City Breeders' Cup Handicap   Luas Line

2006
Park Express Stakes   Danehill Music
Round Tower Stakes   Rabatash

2007
Ballyogan Stakes   Liscanna

12

JESSICA HARRINGTON

Cheltenham, 17 March 2004. Moscow Flyer is odds-on to land the Queen Mother Champion Chase for the second year running and give the Irish a St Patrick's Day big race winner. For much of the race he travels so easily that he is almost running away. Coming to the fourth last fence, on the far side of the course, he is only just behind the leader. He meets the fence all wrong, hits it hard and fires his jockey out of the saddle. A collective groan bursts from the packed stands. Yet, as the horse gallops on riderless, his trainer breathes a sigh of relief.

Jessica Jane Fowler was born in London in February 1947. Although she spent her first two years in England, her family was one of the largest landowners in Ireland. They belonged to a social grouping known as the Anglo-Irish, who usually referred to themselves as Irish but who in the eyes of the locals were English. They tended to live in large houses surrounded by substantial amounts of land which, in some cases, had been given to them in the era of Cromwell. For this reason alone, they tended to be unpopular with the Irish, who burned down some of their houses in the more troubled periods of the twentieth century.

The Fowlers' Irish ancestry does not go back as far as Oliver Cromwell, but it dates back to 1763 when an ecclesiastical member of the family was appointed Bishop of Killaloo. He later became the

Protestant Archbishop of Dublin, and his son married into a family that owned part of the city. Subsequent generations sold this property and bought land in County Meath. At one stage they owned 6,000 acres and, while much of this was later handed over to various tenants on the orders of the Land Commission, they still had more than 800 acres when Brigadier Fowler retired from the British army in 1949.

Brian 'Frizz' Fowler, born in Kells in County Meath, passed out of Sandhurst to join the Royal Artillery halfway through the First World War, and he fought in some of the bloodiest battles in Belgium. A talented horseman, after the war he was appointed an instructor at the army equitation school. He rode in races as an amateur, and he won a silver medal when representing Britain at polo in the 1936 Olympic Games in Berlin. In the Second World War he fought in the desert campaign, seeing action at El Alamein.

He married Mary Walford in 1944. It was the second marriage for his bride, whose first husband had been killed in a plane crash three years earlier. She was left with two young children: Simon, who breeds horses at the Summertown House Stud at Trim in County Meath and was at one time senior steward of the Irish National Hunt Steeplechase Committee; and Sarah, who was to marry Curragh trainer David Ainsworth. Mary Fowler, who lived to be ninety, was also an accomplished rider and won the side-saddle hunter championship at the Dublin Horse Show. Her second husband trained a small number of horses of his own.

Jessica was his second child. John, thirteen months older than his sister, went to Eton but he was not prepared to follow his father into the army and spent six years working for a horse food company. However, he did follow in his father's footsteps when selected for the 1968 Olympic Games in Mexico as a member of the Irish three-day event team. Unfortunately he broke his collar-bone a week before he was due to leave Ireland, and although he made the trip, he was not passed fit in time. It would have been an eventful ride. The cross-country element of the competition took place during a horrific storm and Fowler's intended mount, plus replacement rider, were swept off the course by a torrent of flood water.

Fowler rode in his first point-to-point at the age of sixteen. He became particularly stylish and rode around 260 winners in races, plus over 200 more in point-to-points. In 1976 he won the John Player Amateur Handicap at Galway on Irish Fashion, and his other big race wins included the 1978 National Hunt Chase on Gay Tie and the following year's race on Artic Ale. He also rode the latter to victory in the following month's Topham Trophy over the Grand National fences.

It was also in 1976 that he took over Rahinstown from his father, and two years after that he started training. He has been over-shadowed by the achievements of his sister in recent years, but he won the 1989 Irish Grand National with Maid Of Money after Bankers Benefit was second in the same race two years earlier. Maid Of Money also won successive runnings of the Black and White Whisky Champion Chase at the Leopardstown Christmas meeting, as well as the 1989 Punchestown Chase, while Opera Hat won fifteen races, including the 1998 Melling Chase at Aintree.

Fowler's big race tally would be greater had he not chosen to restrict himself to twenty-one horses, but much of the Rahinstown land is used for farming and the owner does a lot of the work himself. He also allows the Meath and Tara Hunt to use the estate for its annual point-to-point.

Surprisingly, his sister did not go to school until she was twelve. The employment of a governess was not unusual among wealthy families before the Second World War, although it was rare after it, and Jessica shared the services of a full-time professional tutor with the daughter of a friend of her parents. But she was more interested in riding her ponies. 'I grew up with horses, I remember my father playing polo in Phoenix Park and I hunted from a young age. I then started competing in the pony club, and when I was eleven I went to the pony club championships in England. I also showjumped and hunter-trialled.'

When she was finally sent to school, her parents picked out Hatherop, a small boarding school in Gloucestershire. After four years, she went to a finishing school in Paris. A secretarial course followed, and although she then worked part-time as a secretary, she spent much of the week with her horses. She was eighteen when she first rode in the Burghley Horse Trials and twenty when she competed at Badminton, before marrying David Lloyd at twenty-one.

Lloyd was a farmer in the Cotswolds near Cheltenham, and Jessica took two horses from Ireland with her. She hunted with the Heythrop, as did her husband. But, despite her leisurely upbringing, she worked hard on the farm and continued to do so when she had two babies to bring up. However, relations with her husband deteriorated; often Jessica felt that David was not putting in as much work as she did. They split up, after which she worked in a conference centre in Northamptonshire, sometimes in the office and sometimes behind the bar.

Johnny Harrington had first come into Jessica's life when she was eighteen. The son of a Cork paint manufacturer – the firm was Harrington Goodlass Wall – he was educated at Ampleforth and then went into the family business. He left after three years in 1957 with a £750 payoff, and not long afterwards made the mistake of accepting Vincent O'Brien's invitation to spend an evening playing cards. O'Brien was one of Harrington's racing heroes and he felt it an honour to be asked, but his skills at the card table proved expensively inadequate. He left Ballydoyle with his handshake reduced by a third.

However, even in those days he was tremendous company and had a wide circle of friends. He was mad on racing and, through a friend of his father, got a job with Sir Gordon Richards who was then training in Hampshire. He soon realised that he was not cut out to be a trainer, and was offered a job with the Curragh Bloodstock Agency. His likeable manner was a tremendous asset in a business where getting on with people is almost as important as the ability to pick the right horses. Fred Winter took to him and so did Jonathan Sheppard, Fred Rimell and a number of other big names.

He wanted to marry Jessica, a tall and strikingly good-looking girl nearly eleven years his junior, although he felt that her father did not approve of his only daughter linking up with a Catholic horse dealer from Cork. In contrast, John Fowler had married a daughter of the Marquess of Donegal; Harrington was best man on that occasion, and he probably overestimated the Brigadier's objections. After all, he came from what Frizz Fowler would regard as a good family, he had been to 'a good school' and he clearly had a bright future in front of him.

Jessica was keen on Johnny, but not so keen that she preferred him to David Lloyd. However, after her marriage broke up she and Johnny got together again, and one day at Leopardstown he appeared with the leggy blonde on his arm, looking as pleased with himself as if he had just won the Derby. This time it was Jessica's turn to feel apprehensive; she believed that her future mother-in-law took a dim view of her son marrying a Protestant divorcee. The ceremony nevertheless took place in London in August 1976, and the couple went to live at the Commonstown Stud in the County Kildare countryside just above the village of Moone.

Harrington had bought the Georgian house, and its 134 acres, for £80,000 some years earlier. He trained a few horses of his own and kept a couple of mares, but his wife soon turned to eventing once more. Not even the birth of two daughters prevented her achieving considerable success, and she was expected to be chosen as a member of Ireland's three-day event team for the 1980 Olympic Games. However, as with her brother twelve years earlier, fate intervened to prevent her following in her father's footsteps. Russia invaded Afghanistan, and several countries were so incensed that they decided not to send teams to Moscow in protest. Ireland was not one of those countries but the members of the eventing team, and those involved in its selection, shared the views of Great Britain, the USA and others, and they decided not to go.

Instead they went to Fontainebleau on the southern outskirts of Paris for what was dubbed the substitute Olympics. Jessica was picked for the Irish team, which only narrowly failed to win a bronze medal. Riding the same horse, Amoy, owned by her father, she won the following year's international three-day event at Punchestown and in 1983 finished third at Badminton. Her Olympic luck again deserted her at Los Angeles in 1984 – she was selected for the Irish team and flew out to California, only for her horse to go lame – but she rode for Ireland in four European Championships and one World Championship. She also rode in a few point-to-points and the odd bumper, but second was as close as she got.

Her husband's work as a bloodstock agent involved being away from home a good deal, and most of the actual training of his racehorses was done by Eamonn Leigh. A local man, Leigh had started working for Johnny Harrington even before the purchase of Commonstown. During the summer, when Harrington's horses were out at grass, he would often go to England to work for trainers such as John Dunlop and Peter Walwyn. Leigh and his Irish boss had a number of winners in addition to Gay Future's bumper success at Thurles in April 1974. By far the most important came when Hav-A-Heart sprang a 20-1 surprise in the 1985 Irish Lincoln, carrying Jessica's colours.

Two years later Jessica took over the permit. She was becoming increasingly involved and her husband, away on business so often, sometimes found himself unable to recognise one horse from another, much to his wife's amusement. However, the training operation remained on a small scale and winners tended to be scarce. In the 1989/90 season, for example, Crofter's Nest won a maiden hurdle at Wexford and Al Salite one at Leopardstown, but the whole of the following season went by without any addition to the total.

The tide began to turn in the autumn of 1991 when the Earl of

Dunraven asked Jessica to train two three-year-old fillies and run them over hurdles. Both had won earlier in the year, but they were with Flat race trainers on The Curragh. As a permit holder, she was only allowed to train horses belonging to her immediate family, and so she took out a public licence. Lady Olein gave her trainer the initial success in her new role by romping home fifteen lengths clear on her hurdling debut at Leopardstown, with Peter Scudamore in the saddle. Jessica promptly related how she had given her charge plenty of loose schooling, adding that she was a firm believer in the benefits of this practice. It was the sort of remark that might be expected from a trainer who had spent so much of her life concentrating on eventing, and more than one prospective client was sufficiently impressed to send her horses.

Lady Olein won again at Limerick on St Patrick's Day and Mountain Stage, the other Dunraven horse, won a maiden hurdle at Clonmel. In November Lady Olein won twice inside a fortnight at Fairyhouse, including a valuable Grade Three handicap hurdle. People registered that Mrs Harrington could train horses, and they took even more notice the following year (1993) when Brockley Court won five times, including those two November races at Fairyhouse. 'I didn't train that many winners to begin with, but I was lucky enough to have a good horse each year. Lady Olein won some good races, and Brockley Court won at all the right meetings, including some of the televised ones.'

Jessica was bemused, and sometimes irritated, when owners and members of the press telephoned to enquire about her horses and asked to speak to her husband. She thought it was a form of male chauvinism, but it was more that people were used to talking to Johnny, whose friendly manner made even mere acquaintances believe that he was delighted to speak to them. His wife was a comparative stranger from the three-day event world about which they knew little. Furthermore, female trainers were something of a rarity; those members of the media who had had occasion to telephone

Jenny Pitman tended to be left with the impression that they all spoke sharply and all took exception to things you wrote about them.

Only when callers plucked up the courage to speak to Jessica direct did they realise she was not going to bite their heads off. For her part, she became almost as approachable as her husband and was soon on first-name terms with many of her callers. In addition, she never voiced her suspicions of chauvinism to anyone other than her immediate family. Clearly, not all women trainers were in the same mould as the feared Mrs Pitman.

The number of winners from Commonstown steadily increased, from four in Jessica's first season with a licence to twelve in 1993/94. The next season was less than two months old when she went into the history books. Oh So Grumpy, already the winner of one of the feature races at the Punchestown Festival, made her the first woman to train a winner of the Galway Hurdle. She caused considerable mirth in the winner's enclosure with her quip: 'I am not saying who the horse is named after – let's just say it could be a lot of people.'

The gelding boosted his trainer's reputation still further by winning chases at Kempton and Ascot later in the year, by which time the number in the yard had increased to thirty. In January 1996 Jessica Harrington, by now known to many simply as Jessie, became the first woman to train the winner of the Ladbroke Hurdle when Dance Beat won what was then Ireland's richest handicap hurdle race. The mare was ridden by Anthony Powell, who met his death seven years later when his car careered off the road, and across the grass, near the five furlong gate at The Curragh. Powell had enjoyed a close association with the Fowler family: it was he who rode Maid Of Money when she won the Irish Grand National, while he was also on Bankers Benefit when the horse was second in the big Fairyhouse race, and won several races on Opera Hat. He was forty-three, and about to take out a trainer's licence, when he died.

Both Dance Beat and Oh So Grumpy carried the colours of Eileen Queally, whose husband, Peter, became a major investor in Tramore the following year when the County Waterford course was rescued from the predatory arms of housing developers. Peter also gave Jessica and her husband invaluable financial advice in running what had become a business, while his wife's other good horses included Space Trucker. This tough gelding won fifteen races, and in 1999 provided his trainer with her first Cheltenham Festival winner.

The gelding's Grand Annual victory, under Shay Barry, was one of five Irish successes at that year's Festival and helped to compensate visiting punters for the crippling effects of nine Irish-trained beaten favourites. Space Trucker also won the 1996 Fighting Fifth Hurdle at Newcastle and was placed in both the Galway Hurdle and the Champion Hurdle.

But by far the best horse Jessica has trained is Moscow Flyer. The gelding was bought by her husband for 17,000 guineas as an unbroken four-year-old at the 1998 Tattersalls Ireland Derby Sale. He was purchased for Brian Kearney, a Dublin businessman who had never owned a racehorse before and thought it would give him an interest in his retirement. Friends warned Kearney to write off the cost of his investment. Not for one moment did any of them think that his first horse would win him a small fortune.

Moscow Flyer, a strong, lengthy bay gelding, proved unable to win a bumper. This was not a good sign. Most Irish-trained horses who go on to attain top-class status win at least one bumper, although Arkle was a notable exception. However, it was a different story when Moscow Flyer progressed to hurdling. He won his first three races, including the valuable Royal Bond Novice Hurdle at Fairyhouse, although he missed Cheltenham when he was found to have suffered a hairline fracture in his pelvis. This healed remarkably quickly, and he was able to run away with the two-mile champion novice hurdle at Punchestown. Clearly he was Champion Hurdle material, but eyebrows were raised when his trainer decided to take on the mighty Istabraq in the December Festival Hurdle at Leopardstown on New Year's Eve.

The great Champion Hurdler started at 4-1 on, even though the going was so heavy that the race had been postponed from three days earlier. At the final flight Istabraq looked in danger of defeat, and he promptly fell. But his rival's victory was widely regarded as something of a fluke; even his trainer remarked that 'miracles don't happen twice' when assessing her horse's prospects of beating Aidan O'Brien's star in the following month's AIG Europe Champion Hurdle. This time it was Moscow Flyer who fell, but Istabraq again went at the last flight when his rival won the Shell Champion Hurdle.

The following season Moscow Flyer won three Grade One races over fences, including the Arkle Trophy at Cheltenham, although he also fell twice. In the 2002/03 campaign he proved himself the best two-mile chaser by coming home in the Queen Mother Champion Chase. Always travelling well, he won easily by seven lengths. However, he then blotted his copybook by blundering Barry Geraghty out of the saddle when starting at 11-4 on for the BMW Chase. His rider blamed the Punchestown fences, saying 'They are like stone walls. A horse only has to touch one and he's gone.'

Moscow Flyer's performances were having a huge impact on his immediate family. His full sister made a record price for a store filly when knocked down for €215,000 at the Derby Sale and his sire, Moscow Society, also became hot property. He was covering around fifty mares a season when his most famous son started racing, a number that increased to over 130 in two years.

Jessica Harrington also benefited. Her stable grew to such an extent that she was able to run seventy-four horses in the 2002/03 season, and two years later this figure increased to over a hundred. Only Noel Meade and Michael Hourigan ran more.

However, her stable star's jumping was beginning to cause problems. As the press were quick to point out, he would fail to complete the course on every fourth start. Most steeplechasers fall now and again, but for a high-class one to fall so often was rare. It was rarer still for a horse to record such a regular sequence of falls, and it cost Moscow Flyer a second successive Queen Mother Champion Chase. He started odds-on, but it was his fourth start since his last fall and he made a terrible mistake, giving Barry Geraghty no chance of staying in the saddle. 'He was too fresh, and a little bit blasé about the job in hand,' reported the jockey. 'I had too much horse under me and he never settled into a rhythm. He's better off with more racing, and then he's not so full of himself.'

The horse's trainer was inclined to agree, adding: 'Funnily enough, his fall was almost a relief because at least he was all right, and I knew then that there would be another day.'

More racing did indeed prove to be the answer. Moscow Flyer put the hoodoo behind him to regain his Champion Chase crown in 2005, and went on to take the Melling Chase at Aintree. But he never won again, and he was retired after being beaten in the 2006 Queen Mother Champion Chase. He won twenty-six races and more than €1.6 million.

He was a terrific help to the stable, an unbelievable one in fact. If you have one like him, people think you can train, even though most of it is down to the horse. But I do worry with horses as good as him. I go down to the yard in the morning walking on eggshells, hoping that everything is going to be all right. I also get horribly nervous when they run in the big races.

Another to get the Harrington adrenalin going was Spirit Leader, who in the 2002/03 season won the William Hill Handicap Hurdle at Sandown, the Tote Gold Trophy at Newbury and the County Hurdle at Cheltenham. Never before had the same horse won all three of these ultra-competitive handicaps, let alone in the same season. What was all the more remarkable about the mare's feat was that in the first two years of her career she was a frustrating and almost perpetual loser. She won a bumper and a maiden hurdle, but during that period her record read eight second places in nine starts. When horses keep finishing runner-up it can sometimes be because they lack a turn of foot, and are vulnerable to those who can quicken at the end of a race. Usually, however, it is a sure sign that they are ungenuine. It is not always the horse's fault. He or she may have some hard-to-detect physical weakness that causes pain when the horse is asked for maximum effort. Whatever the reason in this case, Spirit Leader came right with a vengeance. The official handicapper assessed her improvement during her big-race winning sequence at more than two and a half stone.

Macs Joy was another notable improver. He went from losing a handicap hurdle in the Leopardstown stewards' room off a mark of 116 to winning the AIG Europe Champion Hurdle with a rating of 156 inside twelve months, picking up the valuable Swinton Handicap Hurdle at Haydock and a €100,000 handicap hurdle at Fairyhouse en route. In 2007 Cork All Star suggested that his name could be one to conjure with by taking the Cheltenham Bumper.

Their trainer has concentrated on National Hunt racing, and for the first few years she had hardly any runners on the Flat. However, the number steadily increased and in 2004 she ran twenty-six horses on the level. Jessica also had her first Flat Group winner when Jazz Princess won the C.L. Weld Park Stakes at The Curragh, although she missed the race: she was a hundred miles away at the Ballindenisk Two-Day Event, at which two of her daughters were riding. All four of her children have ridden eventing.

Anne Marie O'Brien was Ireland's first woman champion trainer before she handed over the reins to her husband, and Frances Crowley (Anne Marie's sister) was the first woman to train the winner of an Irish classic when Saoire, runner-up to Jazz Princess in the Park Stakes, won the following season's Irish 1,000 Guineas. But there have been few other female trainers to reach the top level in Ireland.

'Toby' Wellesley trained classic winners shortly after the Second

World War but in those days women trainers were not allowed, and the official licence holder was a member of her staff. In Britain, top trainers of the fairer sex have also been a rarity, with the notable exceptions of Jenny Pitman and Henrietta Knight. Lynda Ramsden, Mary Reveley and Venetia Williams have also enjoyed considerable success, but there have been few others, although Pam Sly trained the 2006 1,000 Guineas winner Speciosa.

This is one of the great mysteries of racing. Women, by and large possessed of greater sensitivity than men, tend to have a better understanding of animals, and teenage girls are usually more attached to horses than are boys of the same age. Even allowing for the demands placed on them by bringing up children, you would expect more women to make their mark in the training world. Some, who might otherwise have trained in their own name, have been happy to let their husbands hold the licence, but even this does not really answer the unsolved question. For her part Harrington says that being female has caused her no problems as a trainer, and nor were any difficulties placed in her way – those early phone calls apart.

She has yet to win a trainers' championship, but she was second in the lists in the 2004/05 season and she has a good chance of one day winning the title.

I would like to win the Grand National and the Cheltenham Gold Cup. I would also like to win a classic, but that is seriously dreaming! Sometimes I find defeats hard to take but I realise that if you didn't have the defeats you wouldn't enjoy the wins. You have to learn to take the rough with the smooth. Sometimes I get cross and say to myself 'Jesus, everything is going wrong', but then something surprises me, and I find it's all great again. These things tend to level out at the end of the day.

Television viewers were given a fascinating insight into

Harrington's way of life, and the way she handles the ups and downs, when a television camera crew visited Commonstown on several occasions in 2000 to make a documentary series called *Saddle Soap*. It was also shown in Britain under the title of *Turf Wars*. Shots of her swearing when things went wrong on the gallops made for entertaining viewing: 'They were here such a lot that I would forget that the cameras were on me.'

The series gave some idea of how hard Harrington works, but what they did not show was the hour or more that she spends in her office, doing entries and other tasks, before the rest of the staff arrive. Getting up early is her way of keeping on top of the job. Johnny plays his part by helping with the business and financial administration. He also eases the pressure by fielding calls from owners who insist on telephoning late in the evening when the trainer is exhausted.

Her workload has been increased by her determination to serve the interests of her fellow trainers, representing them on the board of Horse Racing Ireland. Many were surprised when she put her name forward in July 2001. She had been appointed to the trainers' seat on the Irish Horseracing Authority, HRI's predecessor, but Willie Mullins, as chairman of the Irish Racehorse Trainers' Association, was the natural choice for the new body. She and Michael Grassick decided to stand against him. Polling was by secret ballot, and a number of trainers were so impressed by what she had done on the IHA board that they went round collecting ballot papers over a wide area. Jessica won the seat by a comfortable majority.

In September 2005 Harrington went on a riding holiday in Kenya with a number of other Irish trainers and their partners, including Arthur Moore, Noel Meade, Willie Mullins and John Fowler – and she broke a bone in her neck.

We were riding across the Laekipia Plains not far from Meru [a remote area well over 100 miles to the north of Nairobi] when my horse stumbled and I went over his head. I knew immediately that something was wrong. I remembered the one thing you should not do in such circumstances is try to move, so I lay still. Fortunately we were only a mile away from an airstrip. The doctors were called and I was flown to hospital in Nairobi.

Johnny, who was taking a break in Portugal, cut short his own holiday and flew back to Ireland. When his wife eventually returned, she was wearing a neck brace. She had to keep it on – as she did a support around the upper half of her body – almost until Christmas. Her period of recuperation coincided with a total loss of form for her horses and she went for eleven weeks without a winner, a losing sequence that was not broken until Studmaster won the Pierse Hurdle in mid-January.

What struck her owners, and her fellow trainers, was the good grace with which Harrington put up with both her own physical discomfort and the agonies of the losing sequence. They knew only too well that they would have been hard pushed to cope so bravely with either.

BIGGEST RACES WON

1994
Galway Hurdle   Oh So Grumpy

1996
Ladbroke Hurdle   Dance Beat

1998
Midlands National   Miss Orchestra

1999

Grand Annual	Space Trucker
Royal Bond Novice Hurdle	Moscow Flyer

2000

Champion Novice Hurdle	Moscow Flyer

2001

Shell Champion Hurdle	Moscow Flyer

2002

Arkle Trophy	Moscow Flyer
William Hill Handicap Hurdle	Spirit Leader

2003

Tote Gold Trophy	Spirit Leader
Queen Mother Champion Chase	Moscow Flyer
County Hurdle	Spirit Leader
Midlands National	Intelligent
Tingle Creek Trophy	Moscow Flyer

2004

Betdaq.com Champion Chase	Moscow Flyer
Melling Chase	Moscow Flyer
Swinton Handicap Hurdle	Macs Joy
C.L. Weld Park Stakes	Jazz Princess
Tingle Creek Trophy	Moscow Flyer

2005

AIG Europe Champion Hurdle	Macs Joy
Queen Mother Champion Chase	Moscow Flyer
Melling Chase	Moscow Flyer

2006

Pierse Hurdle   Studmaster

2007

Cheltenham Bumper   Cork All Star

APPENDIX

BIGGEST RACES WON (to 22 June 2008)

AIDAN O'BRIEN

2007

Nassau Stakes	Peeping Fawn
Yorkshire Oaks	Peeping Fawn
Irish Champion Stakes	Dylan Thomas
Irish St Leger	Yeats
Fillies Mile	Listen
Arc de Triomphe	Dylan Thomas

2008

Prix Ganay	Duke Of Marmalade
2,000 Guineas	Henrythenavigator
Irish 2,000 Guineas	Henrythenavigator
Tattersalls Gold Cup	Duke Of Marmalade
Irish 1,000 Guineas	Halfway To Heaven
Coronation Cup	Soldier Of Fortune
Queen Anne	Haradasun

St James's Palace   Henrythenavigator
Prince of Wales's   Duke Of Marmalade
Ascot Gold Cup   Yeats
Hardwicke   Macarthur

JIM BOLGER

2007

Phoenix Stakes   Saoirse Abu
Moyglare   Saoirse Abu
Goffs Fillies Million   Lush Lashes
National Stakes   New Approach
Dewhurst   New Approach

2008

Derby   New Approach
Coronation Stakes   Lush Lashes

WILLIE MULLINS

2008

Champion Bumper   Cousin Vinny
Ballymore Properties Novices' Hurdle   Fiveforthree

NOEL MEADE

2007

Hatton's Grace Hurdle	Aitmatov

JESSICA HARRINGTON

2007

Beresford Stakes	Curtain Call

BIBLIOGRAPHY

Hannan, Martin, *Rock of Gibraltar* (Cutting Edge Press, 2004)

Holland, Anne, *Horses for Courses: An Irish Racing Year* (Mainstream Publishing, 2005)

O'Brien, Jacqueline and Herbert, Ivor, *Vincent O'Brien: The Official Biography* (Bantam Press, 2005)

O'Neill, Peter and Boyne, Sean, *Paddy Mullins: The Master of Doninga* (Mainstream Publishing, 1995)

Robinson, Patrick with Robinson, Nick, *Horsetrader* (HarperCollins, 1993)

Smith, Raymond, *The High Rollers of the Turf* (Sporting Books, 1992)

——, *Tigers of the Turf* (Sporting Books, 1994)

Sweeney, Tony and Annie, *The Sweeney Guide to the Irish Turf from 1501 to 2001* (Edmund Burke Publisher, 2002)

Williams, Guy St John, *The Racing Lodges of The Curragh* (Daletta Press, 1997)

——, *Winner All Right* (Daletta Press, 1999)

——, *Martin Molony* (Hillgate Publishing, 2001)

Williams, Guy St John and Hyland, Francis P.M., *The Irish Derby 1866–1979* (J.A. Allen & Co. Ltd., 1980)

Williams, Guy St John and Hyland, Francis P.M., *Jameson Irish Grand National* (The Organisation, 1995)

INDEX